LONELY in LOVE

D. River Martin

LONELY IN LOVE
All rights reserved.
Copyright 2021 © D RIVER MARTIN

First Edition
E-Book ISBN: 978-1-7371794-0-5
Paperback: ISBN: 978-1-7371794-1-2

CONTENTS

D. River Martin

PREFACE

I WAS SITTING WITH FRIENDS IN MY WRITING group and happened to share some of the frustrating situations I'd been going through with regards to my partner. They listened kindly, but most responded with some version of "Oh, honey, all men are like that!" Which only served to up my frustration levels because I knew, deep down, that my issues with Gil weren't like most people's.

After a sudden jolt in my relationship with Gil (which I will explain later), I joined several groups on Facebook for non-autistic women (normally called neurotypical or NT), married to someone who is. Formerly, I would have said my partner has Asperger's. In this book, I will use the word autism. Some of the stories within the book will use different words, acronyms, etc., to refer to autism, depending on what the storyteller feels most comfortable with. But don't let all the terminology deter you; this is a book of stories, not a textbook.

Like me, many of the women within the Facebook groups did not become aware of their partner's autism until after they were married or living together. Many of those who *did* know of it felt that it wasn't that big of a deal. Their man was quirky, is all. Gil mentioned the word Asperger's early on in our dating and I thought nothing of it.

As I joined more support groups for women in a relationship like mine, I became engulfed in figuring things out. Not only to help others but to help myself. I was sinking fast with Gil. At first, I thought he was simply different and quirky. I had no idea of the depth that one had to go to understand a man like mine, in order to have a healthy relationship. Or even a tolerable one.

I started to connect with these women on a deeper level because their stories were so like my own. I was hungry for answers. I began to repeatedly hear the same stories, until a pattern emerged. The continual frustration when our friends and family dismissed our concerns, constantly told us to let it go, or to stop being so sensitive. "He's just being a guy" began to make our ears bleed! Or people would say, "My husband does the same things. It's just how they are."

We knew that our men were *not* just like other guys. They were different, and this caused a lot of stress and anguish within the relationship. Each wife/partner wanted to be heard and the outside world wouldn't listen. I found that there was a name for this: The Cassandra Phenomenon.

"The Cassandra phenomenon depicts
a state of confusion, self-doubt, and inner

turmoil that is all too familiar among neurotypical people who, when describing their experiences with an adult on the spectrum, are doubted, discounted, ignored, even rejected by friends, family members, and sometimes professionals who disbelieve their account." (Kenneth Roberson, PhD). Link to website found in the resources section of this book.

Learning about the Cassandra phenomenon, and hearing from other women, began to tug at my heart so deeply that I had to do something. As I became almost addicted to reading these women's posts, I wanted to share their stories with the world.

All stories in this book are from women who didn't share their particular tale with me beforehand. I never mentioned anything about my relationship to them either and yet, the same issues come up for all of us.

Please understand that I am in no way, shape, or form discounting the autistic partner's experiences. In this book, the focus is on the neurotypical partner and her story within a household that is often filled with frustration, grief, and bewilderment, due mostly to misunderstandings on how to relate to her partner.

During a drive on the highway one day—I remember it well—I passed some crash buckets that were put in place to stop a car's momentum if it were to crash into the corner of the divider. I thought about how I needed all that cushioning for my life. I was headed for a crash!

All the stories I had heard rushed to my head and I wanted to scoop them all up and tell the world that we were not crazy! We were suffering and needed support, guidance, and love.

That day, during my nightly Facebooking, I boldly asked the admins of one of the groups if I could invite stories from members and create a book out of them. The admins gave their permission and I received an overwhelming response. *Oh dear!* I thought. *What did I get myself into?* Within a few weeks I had several stories from amazing women who shared their hearts with me. They put themselves out there in order to help, and of course to be heard.

As I read through the stories, not only did specific types of struggle come up repeatedly, I also noticed that the struggle was a daily ordeal. Women were not just telling a story about one incident or venting about one bad day. The bad days were their lives, and they wanted so desperately to be understood. They suffered anguish from the constant proverbial pats on the head, the admonishments to stop being so sensitive, and the 'this too shall pass' drove them to near insanity. And yes, the moment always passes. However, in our world, that moment is repeated again and again.

As I dove even deeper into more and more of the neurodiverse relationship groups, primarily on Facebook, I discovered that not only were women completely frustrated that others might compare their guys to a typical man, they were also very angry and hurt. I saw some begin to lump autistic men in with sociopathic and narcissistic men, and throw away any hope of them being good people. People with a very different way of thinking. People that were doing their best. People that were just as misunderstood as they were. This hurt my soul.

Although sometimes I may want to pull my hair out and jump off a cliff from the frustration I feel with Gil, I never felt he was a bad person. But as I read more stories, I began to get sucked into believing that I was naïve, too kind, that I loved too much. I found myself placed into the category of women who were fools and wondered why I wouldn't leave him. But if a group was there for support, why was I feeling shamed and stupid? For the simple reason that some groups are better than others. So, I ended up focusing primarily on the most supportive group. A group that grew from 300 to 2,000 women in one year, all going through similar situations with their partners. It's profound how many of us are out there and how many more may be unnecessarily suffering, needing answers as I did.

I had many moments of oddity, frustration, disgust, anguish, fear, anger—even throwing a few things—before I knew Gil was on the autism spectrum. Simply knowing that Gil is autistic has changed our lives completely. Knowledge is power. And understanding is how the world finds peace.

"Understanding is the very foundation of love." (Thich Nhat Hanh)

    * In the following stories, names have been changed in order to protect the privacy of those involved.

A JOLT OF REALITY

NEPAL CHANGED EVERYTHING

HE WENT TO NEPAL WITHOUT ME. We'd been together eight years. For years, I had dreamed of the day I would go to an Asian country. I had told him about this dream many, many times.

I was not working and had no family obligations. My schedule was completely open. There would have been no financial strain on his part. He simply *didn't think of me* when he made plans. He let me know a few weeks beforehand, like I was the gardener and pet sitter.

"You need to look after the dogs and feed the birds." He said it matter-of-factly. I was appalled that he was taking off to an Asian country without me. My stomach dropped!!

While in Nepal, he did everything I had always dreamed of doing. He trekked the Himalayas. I love to hike and it's the perfect exercise for my body's aches and pains. He got to walk with elephants, up close and personal, and saw amazing wildlife. Monkeys running loose in the streets and a completely different culture to witness.

And he couldn't understand why I was upset that he went without me. Why I could hardly bear to look at him, or the pictures of his adventures, when he got home. He did everything that I had always dreamed of

11

doing. A chance of a lifetime for both of us to enjoy together. To talk about for years to come. To laugh about that time when . . . but it will never be.

I need him to include me and take me on the next trip. Since he cannot understand why I need it, I must force it. I must make it a demand, which isn't how I want to act in a relationship.

He can't see that he hurt me. But now he's already been to all the Asian countries. Do I make him go again? What if something bad happens and he blames me? Or we make plans while there and he says, "Oh! I've done that and don't want to do that again. You go alone to walk with the elephants." He might say, "You go alone to the temples and gardens." "Take that hike by yourself."

I completely understand how lucky I am that I may get a chance to travel to a distant land. But that longing to simply have a moment to remember, to share that with someone, persists. Those moments when you look at each other and know what each other is thinking . . . I will never have that with him. And I don't plan on leaving him, so I must accept reality or continue to feel anguish about it. It's not easy.

Nepal changed things forever. While he was gone, I went on a search for answers. How could this man that I fell in love with be so cruel? So unaware of my suffering? I am honest and caring; good to him and good for us. We are so compatible physically and spiritually and, I thought, mentally as well. But I second guess that a lot. There is nothing in him that can see how I feel. What was wrong with him?

I looked up traits of those who suffer from narcissistic personality disorder. We have heard a lot about narcissistic people, so I probably don't need to explain it but when I read about it, I realized Gil didn't really fit into the category of narcissism. Although there were similarities, it wasn't a match. Gil may be egocentric, but he's not narcissistic. Gil never did hurtful things to me for his own gain because he always seemed so unaware and shocked when I reacted badly to some of his actions. He was kind and gentle and loving at times, not one to boast or brag, or to be grandiose. He was the complete opposite. He didn't care what he wore and sometimes dressed strangely. He didn't have that swagger a narcissist may have. He did tell me he was always right, but with a bit of a smirk on his face, like a naughty teenager.

I bought a book about walking on eggshells. I often felt that I had to walk on eggshells with him. But not in the way the book described, how someone needs to be careful with a person who has borderline personality disorder. That temperament didn't fit Gil at all. I walked on eggshells with Gil because of his frustration if I hummed or talked on the phone too loudly. I had to follow his schedule, or he would get upset. Those things didn't fit in with the borderline personality disorder. He certainly wasn't a sociopath, although I felt he had no empathy at all for me, because I fell in love with him when he rescued an opossum from his dogs.

He was so sensitive and gentle with animals and a sociopath's most problematic trait is, arguably (from what I have read), their lack of empathy. That wasn't Gil at all; he is sensitive about harm done to others. He would cry at the mere thought of the holocaust or the bomb that hit Hiroshima. Yet, I could cry in front of him and he would disappear like he didn't care, or act oblivious to my emotional issues. I finally stumbled upon a website about people with Asperger's syndrome. They gave examples of how people with this syndrome could be mistaken for being narcissistic or a sociopath or having borderline personality disorder. The site answered all my questions and more. I immediately recognized Gil as having Asperger's syndrome, which is now more commonly referred to as autism level 1.

That trip changed our life together forever. As painful as it was when he left me behind, I am grateful it unfolded as it did. I posted my story soon after finding some Facebook groups for women living with autistic men, and within an hour of posting, a woman who read my post asked me if she could call me. I said yes right away because already, I was connecting with these ladies. She called me late at night and told me that my story was so like hers that her mouth dropped. She felt complete shock! She lived halfway around the world and invited me to live in a home she was renting out and assured me that I would have work and a new start. That was tempting. Although who does that? Who listens to a stranger from halfway around the world, who says to drop everything and go? Wives of autistic men do!! Oh yes! She wasn't a stranger to me. She was me. A sister within a world just like my own.

I didn't take her up on her offer. We still chat from time to time and her place is now rented out, but I wonder how different life would be if I had left. I wonder it still, but I stay.

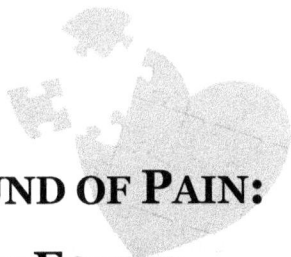

A Merry-Go-Round of Pain:

Lost and Then Found

Margaret's Story

I met him when I was seventeen. He was twenty-two and he was *so* handsome. And basically, the leader of the group of older kids I had just started hanging around with. He owned his own home, and we would go over there to party. I was smitten! I was fresh out of reform school and a senior in high school. I obviously had a troubled childhood and adolescence (that I don't need to go into here). I was looking for a safe place of belonging.

Looking back, I can see how 'primed' I was to be blinded to this condition of high-functioning autism. He wears a charming mask. I had absolutely no clue of what his hidden condition would mean in terms of its impact on my entire relational life until recently. I'm fifty-seven years old. A mother of two grown children. A practicing psychotherapist for thirty years! A driven, independent, and passionate woman, who ended up basically being a single parent, living alone and overburdened in a loveless marriage for over twenty-five years.

I stumbled onto this knowledge through a patient of mine. She has no clue about this, but she introduced me to the concept of her 'Aspie' (being married to somebody that looks on the outside to be charming or successful, only to have a set of traits and deficits in functioning that would cause his wife to cry alone in her bed, ripping hairs from her body due to her inner pain and frustration).

As she talked through her issues about her husband with me, red flags started going off in my brain. This sounded like *my* life! I began to do research into this relatively new field of understanding, the neurotypical (NT) and high-functioning autism (HFA) couple. I am a marriage and family therapist myself. Please understand this: I have over 5,000 supervised hours of couples and family therapy training under my belt! And I have been practicing for thirty years now. But I was never trained in this because it is relatively new in terms of being understood as a *thing*. Talk about a blinding light bulb moment! Holy Batman! How could I have missed this?!

It all started to make sense. His methodical, 'logical' speech patterns. The circular fights we would have that never got us anywhere. The complete lack of physical and emotional intimacy. The fact that he has no friends and would fight me tooth and nail anytime I wanted to have a social event. How he would blame me, gaslight me into believing I was crazy, unloved because I was unlovable, too demanding or hard to please. His severe procrastination and hoarding behaviors. Watching the same TV show or movie repeatedly (can't we *please* watch something else for a change?)

It also made sense how none of the therapy I have dragged him to over the years ever worked. Those well-meaning but uninformed therapists would operate on the premise that we had a reciprocal or equal pattern in our marriage, when in fact that was not the case! He's autistic, but you would never know it unless you *knew* it! *Yes, I was* functioning as the only adult in the family and had all the resentment and burden that comes with doing all the

16

heavy lifting! I was forced to be—because I did not want this, I did everything I could to change this—the breadwinner, child care provider, home and vacation planner, investment officer, etc.

I asked him for what I needed. I was patient and kind (for a while). I tried to be inviting and encouraging, not controlling. But nothing worked. As I became more stressed out and overwhelmed, he shut down and justified his disengagement more and more. He drank, spent hours on the computer gaming, developed a porn addiction. The gap widened, and resentments grew as the space between us got ever larger. His best defense was a good offense. Turn it around on me and invalidate me until I acted crazy, then he could point the finger at me because in fact, I had become crazy.

Sadly, our kids watched this defensive absentee husband/father and stressed-out 'psycho mom' as their role models. I will say that he was much better with the kids. He coached their sports and drove them endlessly. He was more of a friend to them than a father. But to me, he was a nightmare.

Admittedly, there is probably more going on here than simply autism. But all these issues seem to blend into one mess of a person and husband.

You may ask why I didn't leave him? I have asked myself this question as well. I think it was a combination of things: Believing it might be my fault, low self-esteem, not wanting to raise my kids in two separate homes. And ultimately, I knew that I would *still* be responsible for everything, and for two homes, and paying alimony on top of managing everything myself anyway. I really think it would have been just as bad, but in a different way, had I left. The kids would have blamed me and somehow it would have wound up to be all my fault.

I'm working on damage control for all of this now,

but I really wish I had known long ago what was going on in my life. I feel validated having answers that make sense to me now, and that gives me some direction for my healing. And I have a wonderful personal therapist who keeps me grounded and moving forward. But it has been a long, hard road. And I would have done many things differently if I had known then what I know now.

This revelation has only come to me in the last year. I am trying to incorporate this understanding into a transformation. I was primed for these dynamics because I was raised with these dynamics in my family of origin. Sadly, I'm sure I have passed on to my children the unfinished business of my own life. I'm sorry they have picked up my baggage, but I am working on it the best I can. Fortunately, they are doing well and beginning to create their own lives. I have hinted to my husband that I think he may have elements of autism, but I've never addressed it directly. He is sixty-two years old and I don't think it is likely that he will change.

I'm tired of fighting. I want to direct my energy into myself at this point of my life. The change must come from me, from my own self-compassionate understanding of what it means to have lived the life I have chosen, unfortunately, with my eyes half-closed. I must now make peace with resentments. Open new doors of opportunity for myself. Be more gracious with myself and those around me in new ways. This revelation has been liberating, sober, painful. And incredibly positive.

I chose at this point not to divorce. There are many reasons for this and it's a very personal decision. I am living my life in a more fulfilling way and I am comfortable with this choice.

Today I try to look at humanity on more of a spectrum of diversity, and neurologically is just one lens to view things through. It's a new journey and I am just beginning. I send LOVE to all my fellow travelers on this uncharted road. I wish for you, your own compassionate understanding, and the ability to heal and re-direct your life in a way that makes sense to you.

* * *

River's comments:

MARGARET'S STORY brings to the table information, validation and hope.

Within my neurodiverse relationship groups, it's common to hear about getting therapy and how traditional marriage and family therapists can do more harm than good. Before I knew Gil was on the spectrum, we went to three therapists and each one asked us to do certain things. For instance, Gil and I were asked to write down three things every day that we appreciated about one another. I wrote down my three things and he did not. Each day I wrote them down and each day he did not, which filled me up with more and more frustration. I finally wrote down things about myself for him to write down. He still would not do it! At the time, of course, not knowing the root cause of why he could not or would not write down three things, made the situation worse and made him look like a complete jerk—like he couldn't think of or take the time to write down something nice about me.

A person on the autism spectrum usually finds it very hard to step outside of their routine and look to what another person is doing. It now makes sense why he probably couldn't grasp the idea of writing something like that down. The exercise also led Gil to call the therapy stupid. But I kept trying to get answers, so I found another traditional therapist. This one gave Gil some homework: he was to come home from work and ask me how my day was. That never happened. It was suggested that we spend a half-hour a day to sit down and talk to each other without the TV or phones on. That also never happened. Well, it would take place if I forced it, and that always led to Gil walking away from me when I was in the middle of a heartfelt story.

Finally, a therapist mentioned that we plan a trip together. Now, I could write another book on that one. Trips away and plan them together? I laugh! I must plan the entire trip and he follows, which leads to me doing all the work to make the trip enjoyable for him, leaving me, in return, with feelings of resentment. He is getting slightly better with trip plans now, but only after we found a therapist that understands autism to guide him on the subject. So, you get my point on traditional therapy? It doesn't work, and in my case, it did more harm than good. It was a waste of time and money, but it also caused me to think that I was the problem. Maybe I was too sensitive? He is 'just being a guy'! I'm stupid not to leave him. Etc.

And since I bring that up, why didn't I just leave him? You may ask why on earth women stay in a relationship with such chaos, and sometimes real mental harm inflicted on all involved? I have several different thoughts on that. I will break it up into two categories. The women who are unaware their husband has autism, and those that know they do and stay anyway.

Women have told me that when, like myself, they didn't know in the beginning, they thought *they* might be the problem. Exactly how I felt as well. Many women attract these types of men into their lives when they might be struggling financially, or they may have been through a difficult divorce etc. In my case, Gil swept me off my feet when I was financially desperate. So, life might be awful, and these guys, a lot of the time, are very childlike and refreshing. They are forthright and seemingly very honest, which makes them very attractive to a woman who might be beaten down by this world.

But there are also many women who have a great life and good career who fall fast for a man with autism! The honesty and blunt nature are attractive. I think a woman who is doing well might also like a man with autism because they don't ask for lots of their time. At least mine never has. They don't demand your time like a lot of NT men might. They probably won't ask a lot of questions about your life either, which can also be refreshing. They live on a schedule, which is often admirable and predictable. And some are great at wearing a mask. Like my Gil. He is well known and is part owner of a good-sized company, and he was sweet and totally focused on me in the beginning. Oh, he knew how to snag a girl.

But as time goes on, even the most well put-together woman will get baffled by her man's charm disappearing quickly. The honeymoon period ends and when things get real, they get very real. Then, when issues arise, the autistic partner will often turn to 'gaslighting' or manipulation and anyone can get turned upside down by that, fast.

I remember screaming at Gil, asking him, "What's wrong with you?" And somehow it always got turned back onto me. Something must be wrong with me. So basically, my theory as to why a lot of women stay, is that they get blindsided and begin to question themselves. By the time they might figure it out, they have made their house a home and they may have young children to raise. They also may feel trapped financially or they are providing for their autistic husband/partner and don't want to up and leave him. They may have moved for their guy and have no family support close by. They may not want to break their marriage vows. There are lots of reasons a person may not leave, and a big one for some women is fear of their children being left alone with their husband if custody is shared.

And for women that make the decision to stay even though they are financially stable, kids have grown, maybe not married to their guy, and could leave easier than most . . . I think, for the most part, that they may be plumb tuckered out! Some, such as Margaret and myself, have made an educated decision to stay because we went lots of years not knowing and survived. Margaret was able to do it and raise wonderful children as well. I often say to myself that I'm not starting all over again with someone new, or living single and all that trouble again. I'm tired!! Done! I completely respect Margaret's educated choice to stay.

When I finally found out that I wasn't completely nuts, I saw my Gil in such a different and new light that it was like a dark cloud lifted. I wanted to finally see all that I had been missing. Let me explain that. It's been almost three years now since Gil was diagnosed. I've accelerated my learning from writing this book and talking to amazing women like Margaret. Often, when they're in a neurodiverse relationship unknowingly, wives/partners of autistic men say they feel they lost their soul.

Once they find out and learn more and more about their guy, they go through grief and it's hard, and many understandably leave, but for those that don't and who get past the grief, it's like a whole new world opens. For me, I began watching lots of cartoons. Sounds crazy but I wanted that child side back, and for love and tenderness to start to run through my veins again. I watched nothing but funny movies. I focused on me and wrote a children's book. My dream of doing that came true!! I started to lighten up on things, and find what I had been missing for so long while I was immersed in trying to figure out my man's world. I also found myself falling in love with Gil all over again in a different way. Not infatuation or all the strange things I thought I admired in him before, but a deep compassion for him instead of anger for the often-hurtful words and negativity that he filled my ears and the house with. I also began to take charge. I did plan a trip and sure, I had some hard moments with him, but I could let it go in order to enjoy our trip as best possible.

Knowledge of his autism diagnosis gave me power! The power to say no to his negative comments, along with the understanding that he wasn't taught how to navigate his thoughts and words any better. The power to let him know when he was hurtful and let it go. The power to be myself and take care of myself so I could be a strong force for this kind of one-sided relationship I was in, and am still in. One-sided as in, he cannot give me what a relationship usually looks like.

Having the knowledge to understand Gil forces me to be okay with me, and not lean on a man for my self-worth. So, with all that, I like it more and more. And, here's the best part. The more I become myself, the more he starts to follow. If I eat better, then he starts to eat better. I talk with a softer voice, he begins to talk a little—and I say just a little—more softly, with kindness. Sure, there will always be moments that are mind blowing and frustrating and most would never live one second in a household like mine, but it's so much better than it was. It's better because I have changed my thinking. I know he can't change much. And that's okay. But he does change little by little and it's very endearing to me that he does try now. When I am telling him a heartfelt story, I may have lost him, but he doesn't get up and leave until I am finished talking. That is a very good thing. And I asked myself this: Why leave now after all the pain and torture, when I'm finally seeing some light and happiness?

Those are my thoughts. And I also must add that there are autistic quirks, and then there is downright abuse too. These men are not exempt from being abusive. They are people just the same and if you experience fits of rage that are not controllable or there is physical harm to you or your children, please seek help immediately.

There are certainly bad people in this world. No doubt. But the 'bad' isn't autism.

I've had many conversations with our counselor who understands autism, and my understanding is that of course, we all have our dark sides. Gil may say words that I take to be discounting or even cruel. But I would never say he is a bad person. I also believe, and I could be wrong, that many who are not diagnosed young might develop mental challenges and personality disorders. Gil has signs of narcissism, mainly a big ego, and that doesn't make him a bad person. Gil grew up in a home that didn't understand autism or even know it existed; not only that, but his environments both at home and at school weren't accepting of differences and didn't allow him to develop good practices from the start. I feel that for Gil, the autism often softens or makes the underlying issues more transparent. Yet, Gil is a good guy, big ego, autism and all.

D. River Martin

MEET THE KIDS

LYNN'S STORY

WE BEGAN DATING IN 2011. We had so much in common. We both had been married for twenty-three years before divorcing and we each had two college kids, all about the same age. It felt great to spend time with a guy who appreciated so many things about me. At least, he showed great appreciation for them at the time. He admired my career, loved meeting my friends and family, and said that he was thankful for the care I put into making special meals or plans for us. There weren't really any red flags in the beginning. He was wonderful.

Charles was the first man I had dated that really seemed interested in hearing about my career and my role as a mother. We spent a lot of time together. And it was more than us being together. He became involved with my friends, work people, kids, etc. He fit in easily. My friends found him interesting and he was like a walking encyclopedia with a sense of humor.

I'd been around Charles's son David several

27

times. He was awkward, talked nonstop at a million miles an hour, and usually ended up over-sharing things most people would be embarrassed to admit. Like that he was wearing jeans that hadn't been washed in two years. I thought he was only nervous about being around someone that was not his mom. He was also hooked on one subject at a time. One that I remember most, was a fascination with the cheapest places to eat out.

Charles's daughter Nancy I had met for the first time at dinner a month before Christmas. Charles and I drove out to where she attended college. We met at a restaurant, where Nancy proceeded to bury her face in her phone the entire dinner, and when she looked up to engage in conversation with her dad, it was to discuss hockey. There was nothing comfortable about being around Nancy. She was very critical of almost everything around her. She didn't have a network of friends, or even one friend for that matter.

By Christmas, Charles and I were spending a fair amount of time together. My kids alternate between spending time with their dad or me for the week before Christmas. That year, they spent Christmas Day through New Year's Day with their dad, so I was going to be without kids. Charles asked if I would mind hosting his kids and their significant others with him at my place, since it would accommodate that number of people and my home was fully decorated for the holidays. I was happy to host. Charles shared with me his struggles with Christmas since his divorce because his apartment, although very nice, was small and he didn't decorate. His kids seldom went there to visit. He felt like this would be an opportunity to establish post-divorce traditions with his kids. We both felt confident this would be our first of many holidays together.

I was happy to help with Christmas and felt like a pro because I had kids the same age and could relate. Charles asked if they could stay for two nights since they were driving a good hour to come, and he really wanted to spend time with them. The plan was that I would do a nice Christmas dinner (beef tenderloin with all the trimmings) along with all the fine touches I love to do as a hostess, and Charles would take us all out for dinner the second night.

David and his girlfriend arrived exactly on time (he is always punctual). Nancy came about two hours late. When I realized she was going to be late and we had no idea when she would arrive, I tried to save the seventy-five-dollar tenderloin I had bought and not ruin the dinner or the night.

Nancy finally arrived, with her boyfriend, and didn't apologize for being late. We sat down for dinner and enjoyed our meal. Charles asked lots of questions, and he spent a lot of time pulling words from Nancy's mouth. It was painful to watch. After dinner we moved to the living room to open gifts. I had small gifts for Charles's kids and their boy/girlfriend. I honestly didn't expect them to buy me anything more than a hostess gift. Something that you would bring to anyone who hosted you for dinner, like a poinsettia or a candle. David and his girlfriend brought me wine and coasters. I knew his girlfriend picked them out because she shared the story behind the gift. It was thoughtful. Nancy came empty-handed and thought nothing of it. Charles put a lot of effort into buying her gifts. Most of them were hockey themed. She showed almost no emotion while opening them.

The following morning everyone except Nancy and her boyfriend got up around 9 AM. I made French toast and bacon along with coffee and juice. We all enjoyed breakfast. When Nancy and her boyfriend finally appeared around 11 AM, Nancy sat on the couch next to me. I asked her not once, not twice, but three times if she wanted coffee. The third time I had to say, "Nancy, I'm asking you if I can get you coffee or juice."

She looked at me and asked, "What?" in an agitated tone. I felt embarrassed.

The remainder of the day was spent with David chirping like a bird nonstop and Nancy borderline self-absorbed, on her phone and sniping at her boyfriend. It was painful for me to be around.

After they left, I mentioned to Charles how surprised I had been by the 'coffee exchange'. His response: "I didn't hear that." I was hurt and shocked. He'd been sitting within four feet of Nancy and me.

He began trying to explain Nancy and her tardiness and how she can be self-absorbed. That she's a new college student away from her boyfriend, and on and on. He did tell me he was not happy with her behavior, but it was not something that was addressed in the moment. Charles spoke with Nancy's mom and her response was along the lines of: she couldn't believe that I was upset about not getting a gift and that I was petty. I wasn't as upset about the gift as I was with Nancy's behavior. The mom didn't respond to that part at all, or maybe she wasn't told about that side of it. I had to let it go.

For the following six years Charles defended, explained, and tried to teach me why his kids behaved the way they did.

It wasn't until 2018, in marriage counseling, that our therapist told me she believes Charles may be on the high-functioning end of Autism Spectrum Disorder (ASD) and that both of his kids are affected too. It was like a light went off. It explained so many interactions and so many non-interactions. All those years not knowing put so much unnecessary strain on our relationship. I had to let that part go and start fresh. So far so good.

* * *

River's comments:

LYNN SHARES with us a common theme that occurs with an autistic partner when we don't understand autism. She's introduced to a new family member that shows signs of autism, yet Lynn is in the dark at the time, trying desperately to make Christmas a good time for all.

Lynn expressed something that all partners of autistic men want to hear and feel: validation and clarity. Did Charles's daughter Nancy sound like a bratty teenager? Sure, she did for the most part. But the extreme of her behavior is well depicted in Lynn's story. Also, the excuses both the mom and dad gave for her behavior is often typical when just trying to cope. At least I've experienced this with teens. But most importantly, Lynn's story is a small glimpse into the world of not understanding autistic behavior and the hurt and pain that can be caused by the lack of understanding. There is a world of autistic people out there wanting desperately to be understood and loved and to make connections, just as neurotypicals do, but excusing bad behavior does nothing to help.

Maybe Nancy is used to people thinking she is weird if she engages? Maybe she's angry at the world for treating her badly because she is different? Although David seemed much different from his sister. This is a reminder that the spectrum is vast and much depends on the individual. We have heard time and again with autism that if it's not caught early in life and they're not given guidance toward appropriate behavior (according to their level and in language they understand), most will tragically grow into very angry and lonely adults. They will be isolated in a world that doesn't understand them.

Also, many parents of autistic girls say that it was a long, hard road to getting their daughters diagnosed. Autism presents differently in girls and goes undiagnosed in them more often.

Lynn said how shocked and hurt she was that Charles didn't support her or see what she was witnessing in both of his children—what she considered to be bad behavior. Excuses or not, the behavior was beyond being young or stressed. Charles kept defending them, which is understandable maybe at first, yet after many years he couldn't truly see what Lynn had gone through with them. He provided no support for Lynn when the children's mom thought Lynn was being rude.

I consistently hear this from women living with autistic men: their partners do not stick up for them or stand by their side. A sense of being 'on the outside' is common in neurotypical partners, not only for a new partner coming in, but even for a partner that's been around for several years.

I also met Gil late in life, as Lynn did with Charles. Even though I don't have children of my own, Gil has an adult son. As I read Lynn's story, I remembered the sting of not feeling that Gil had my back. With both of our parents gone and most of Gil's family living out of state, I tried for us to be less alone by connecting with his son's mom's side of the family. This was risky, trying to connect with the ex, but there was no one else close by and Gil still had holiday dinners with them from time to time.

At first it seemed that all was okay, and they were welcoming, but as time went on, a shift happened and they disappeared. I stupidly kept trying to fit in and be 'a part of' and that only made things much worse. I must mention that I also was desperate for connection since the family had known Gil many more years than I had. I had hoped they'd help me to understand him better. Gil never seemed to care, and I felt he sided with them. Like Lynn, I

33

didn't understand autism, so we made honest and understandable mistakes. I continue to feel ousted from Gil's close family and it's tragic to me. It's actually been one of the driving forces to get this book out, so this doesn't happen to other families.

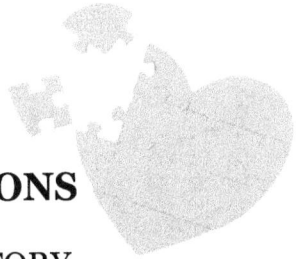

TRANSITIONS

CLAIRE'S STORY

I'VE BEEN MARRIED TO MY HUSBAND for twenty-four years. We dated for two years before we married. We have two children. A boy and a girl who are now grown. Our son is diagnosed with high functioning autism and goes to counseling. My husband is not officially diagnosed but has all the signs of autism.

This is a story about a single decision that sent my family into a tailspin of difficult events. My husband, a Certified Public Accountant, did—and continues to do—very well in his profession with numbers, correctness, and having everything under control with little to no emotion. His profession is perfect for him, and his high IQ guided him to a specific aspect of accounting that made him very financially successful. Although the more successful he became, the more he had to deal with people. His clients were a great challenge for him. He was forced to get out of his comfort zone and talk with people.

One of his great achievements was when he signed a contract with a very lucrative client that greatly enhanced his good reputation, but also took

35

him away from other areas of his job and other clients. Within a year, this major client offered him a position with their company.

They said, "We need you and we would like you to become part of our staff." It was a great position with more money. Accepting the position meant that he would have to make changes in his routines, sit in a big office with bright lights and lots of people around and the worst part, he would need to talk to other co-workers. He declined the position and lost his account, leaving him with even less money than he had been earning before.

His decision to stay with his company and earn less pay now led to consequences that affected the whole family. At first, we didn't take that into consideration because we didn't understand how much it would affect us. A little less pay, we thought, would be okay if we cut back on expenses a bit. I supported his decision because I knew how difficult it was for him to work with others. I thought it was just an adjustment period in spending less, and in the end, everything would be okay.

My biggest mistake was misjudging the adjustment period because for him, it felt like total chaos. He didn't know how to deal with the change. It was very difficult for him to earn less money. He was frightened that he'd made a poor decision in not taking the job and he pushed his family too much, making us change—much more than we needed to— the lifestyle we were used to.

He was so focused on cutting expenses that

every single purchase had to be justified, and he tried to explain to us every single time why we had to be careful with money. Like we were stupid. He was a jerk to us for what seemed (to us) no reason, because the situation really wasn't as difficult as it felt to him. What was most problematic was, simply, the autism. He got so focused on feeling stuck and saving money that he forgot to improve his business by getting more clients. He only focused on the purchases, and cutting expenses within the family, more so than his business. I felt miserable and at a loss of what to do. I lived under so much pressure that I considered divorce. Our daughter suffered as well, feeling that she contributed to the money stress, and she considered dropping out of college. Luckily, she didn't drop out and continued her studies and graduated.

The financial situation was far from being as serious as he made it out to be. My second mistake was that I didn't realize he was so rattled by the changes in routine. I attempted to talk to him and I'm glad that I did. I asked him if our situation was so serious? Was there something he was not telling me?

"I don't think things are that bad," I told him. "We still have money coming in and we have managed to cut extra expenses." He and I had a long conversation, and both of us realized he was having an autistic reaction to change, and he understood that his reaction was making the entire family miserable.

We worked on his challenge with change and on our relationship. It wasn't easy but we worked on it one day at a time. Sometimes one moment at a time. He needed to process it in his own time. He also tried to make changes in his relationship with our daughter. She had distanced from him for a long time because of the constant frustration he caused her about money and other issues. He realized he had hurt her in doing this.

It took us all almost a year to feel like a family again. I felt so lonely during that time. Nobody understood because they couldn't understand that he was not being a jerk on purpose. I couldn't share with anybody what was going on. During especially difficult days, I had to rely on my knowledge and faith to move forward alone as best I could, with no shoulder to cry on. He felt lonely also, and pressured because everyone was relying on him to do better. He and I disconnected emotionally even more than before the changes. He noticed that I was miserable about this disconnect but didn't really understand why, or how to handle it. Instead of being able to talk to me about it, he thought I didn't love him anymore and I would be better off on my own. He didn't realize he was pushing us so much.

Today, I think we are over the worst of it and doing better. I made changes in my career to earn more income for the family. I realized what was happening to him, and that understanding helped pull us through. I helped him as best I could to re-focus on his job instead of finances by continuing to remind him what was important, and he did better.

I told him how this situation affected the whole

family, directly and with no emotions involved, thinking that to be the best way to talk to him, but it only made things worse. I think he felt I was too demanding. I suggested counseling so that he could understand more fully what happened, but he doesn't believe in counseling. For him, talking to a stranger about personal matters is not acceptable. But he doesn't mind if I go.

Instead of counseling, I joined a support group online. This meant that I could talk with real people, living through similar things as I was. So far, it's been helpful and I'm learning a lot from hearing the stories from other women married to autistic men.

If you were to ask me how I'm feeling right now, it would be difficult to answer. I'm working on taking care of myself. I'm going to the gym. I try to meet with friends regularly. I think I'm still sad, but I don't want to give in to more sadness. If the future brings the same challenges with work again, I'm sure that he will react the same as before. He is not able to learn from it. He can learn from social situations, not to say something to a stranger because it's rude, or not to make jokes when someone is telling something serious, etc. But with work, he can't change his perception. He can't work with co-workers without having lots of stress that he brings home with him. I hope I am better prepared, in case of a similar situation, if a change of routine arises because I know it will happen again and again.

* * *

River's comments:

CLAIRE'S STORY is such an inspiration to me because she took each day, and sometimes each moment, to get through the tough times when her hubby earned less income. She pinpointed that autistic reaction to change and worked with him, instead of creating more chaos by getting angry and fighting the situation.

When she said she was still sad today, I understood. A normal day with a partner on the autistic spectrum is not normal to the average neurotypical couple. I have heard from women living with autistic men that we must remind ourselves that, on a good day, our life is as normal as it's going to get.

I love Claire's last paragraph when she talks about taking care of herself. This is key for all of us, but it can be certainly life-saving for a partner living with an autistic man. Our husbands/partners simply *cannot* give us that emotional support that women need from their partner. We must search for it elsewhere. Either by working out and meeting people at the gym or releasing those endorphins in other ways, for when we get home, we may have to handle a meltdown. Be it joining a group of women or a walking group, something that gets us out in the world is good. It's very easy to get swept up in always thinking of our men.

A year after she wrote this story, I emailed Claire to ask how she was doing. She sent me a quick message that said:

Last year was a learning path for me. He is now officially diagnosed, and it helped him to really accept his condition. When I tell him "You are acting like an Aspie right now," he stops and listens. (River's note: Aspie is a nickname for Asperger's—some people find it offensive but it's often used affectionately by family members of autistic people.)

Also, I adopted all the techniques my son's psychologist recommended, such as short sentences. Talking in such a way that he doesn't feel accused. Giving life challenges that arise in small doses for him, and so on.

I also make sure I have the means to take care of myself. That I am prepared with time to engage in activities that I enjoy. I take care of my friends and give more time and dedication to my friendships.

And the most important is that I don't worship him! He might be very intelligent with numbers, but he is completely illiterate in social situations and totally dependent on me in that department. Instead, I try to worship myself.

Claire's attitude and understanding are admirable. She understands that she is also an amazing force in the relationship. Her talk of worshipping him I know all too well. Gil, being a boss at work and having traveled the world, etc. gave me a great ego boost! Of course, this made it even harder when I learned that he wasn't 'all that', as I am sure was the case for Claire as well.

41

Wives/partners of autistic men go through a grieving period when they find out their men aren't who they thought they were. They are so honest and forthright in the beginning and things change once we dig in and live with them. And, sure, this happens after the honeymoon period for most couples but for us, there is another level of sadness. They don't show love in the same way as we do, or fulfill our needs as we feel they should. We can't just get in a fight and expect it to be better later. It's a constant struggle to communicate and live together.

Not all autistic men bring home the big paycheck. Some wives/partners of these men support their husbands, and I'm sure that causes other problems. I love how Claire mentions how we often are needed. To give them a life they could never have. A life of understanding, love, of having a family and a life outside of work. And now Claire has more relationships outside of the home as well, because she kept fighting to understand her man and her place in the marriage and in her life.

Claire's wisdom on this aspect is that she understands that he can work on his behavior but not his thinking. She understands that, simply, he is who he is. He is her husband and the father of her children and he has something different about him that we call autism.

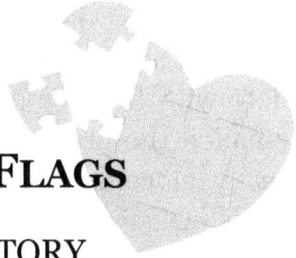

MANY RED FLAGS

AMANDA'S STORY

I'M A MARRIAGE AND FAMILY THERAPIST and if a potential neurotypical client came to me wanting help with a husband who is on the high functioning end of the autistic spectrum, I must be honest and say that I would refer her to another therapist. I can delve into a troubled traditional/neurotypical marriage with open arms, but not a neurodiverse one, even though I live in one every day. The tools of the trade that I've learned as a marriage and family therapist don't come close to helping a neurodiverse couple to live a happy and healthy marriage.

I met my husband through Match.com. We were both thirty-five years old. I was just coming out of a very bad, emotionally abusive relationship and was not myself. I had extremely low self-esteem. I was desperate to get married and felt I'd already found true love twice, but life circumstances had made those relationships not work out. So, I wasn't expecting to find my soulmate again because I'd already had that, and I just wanted to get married. I didn't care much about amazing romance or being swept off my feet.

My first date with Jeremy, my future husband, was at a coffee shop. I hadn't planned on going on a date with him for quite some time yet, but we had emailed the previous day almost all day long and I really felt connected to him. He talked about his work goals. He was smart and witty and funny in the emails. He told me that he was in the military, so I knew, job-wise, there was the safety and security that I was looking for. Ironically, he knew some people who I worked with and our jobs were only two blocks apart from one another. Small world. It seemed like a meant-to-be, kind of perfect match to me.

Even though my self-esteem was so low, he genuinely wanted to spend time with me, which I felt was amazing because he was smart and witty and handsome and still wanted me. When he wanted to meet me, he didn't pester me to do so and let me take my time. He allowed me the space to let him in when I wanted. That was something I wasn't used to. Before, I'd had the kind of guy who smothered me or only popped up when it was convenient for him and expected me to be at his beck and call.

When Jeremy and I met at the coffee shop, there were some red flags right away, but I brushed those off because there were other great qualities that I saw in him. The actual red flags were also hidden, in a way, because I liked his awkwardness in public. For instance, when we ate out, he didn't talk, and he often didn't seem to have any social manners. It was subtle but I could tell that he was different. He would keep his eyes down, which was a bit annoying and a first red flag, but I ignored it. One time when we were out for yogurt, he finished his yogurt very fast and was out the door before I finished mine. I liked that he wasn't afraid to do what he wanted to do, but it was odd. I didn't know then that it was the crowded yogurt shop that made him feel uneasy and that he needed to leave as soon as possible.

His humor was different than I had known as well. He sometimes called my clothes grandma clothes even though they were very nice work clothes that I got compliments on all the time from colleagues. I dismissed that comment because I thought he was trying to be funny and not put me down. They were nice clothes, so it was a kind of playful humor, like maybe he felt under-dressed next to me or something. And the way he said it was so matter-of-fact that it didn't really come off as rude. I didn't realize then that he was putting me down and thinking that was funny. After a while of him continuing this kind of rude joking, it was not funny anymore, but I dealt with it and tried to ignore or excuse it by brushing it off as something he'd picked up in the military.

I liked how simply he dressed in his shorts and T-shirts. I'd been with guys before that were very vain and cocky. Of course, now, Jeremy will wear shorts the second he gets home, even through the winter. He only ever wears work/combat boots or sneakers. He wears certain socks and certain shoes and certain brands of workout clothes, never trying new brands. I guess I went from one extreme to the other. I didn't like the overly dressed, must-look-good guy so went to the 'I only dress how I want to' guy.

During our first couple months of dating, he never told me that he had five dogs. Seeing his house for the first time was not what I wanted to see. Very dirty, and the dogs were not trained. They took over and were very spoiled. They are still unruly dogs because he treats them as spoiled little children. The dogs have been an issue since the first time I met them. They are so ill-tempered and it's frustrating because they could be better if they had a better owner. He won't allow any training for them. So, when they misbehave, I get angry and my frustration overflows because just a little training would go a long way. Five dogs are a lot and they need training, but he won't allow it.

He also hid the fact that he was a 'gamer' and this was a huge red flag for me, but I was too deep into the relationship when I finally found out to have that issue stop us. I thought, *It's just gaming, we can overcome this one.* Before he and I were living together, he would often not answer the phone on Sundays, and I just thought this was odd. I would want to stop by with dinner and he would say, "No, I'm good." It was a shock that he didn't want me to stop by to see him because on all other days he seemed to truly want to see me. Only when I moved in did I learn why. I realized how big he was on routines, and that spending time alone was a necessity. He would play his video games all Sunday long.

When I moved in, he would ignore me and the dogs for the whole day to play video games. One of the biggest fights we ever had was over his gaming and ignoring me and even ignoring sex as well. Intimacy was happening less and less. Him ignoring me all day, and sometimes for several days, was upsetting. I asked him if he wanted gaming over sex with his new love. Were his schedules so important that I didn't exist anymore? I began to think that he did not like sex. I thought maybe he was gay. I looked up books for guys with low sex drive. He didn't initiate and didn't seem to care if we had sex or not. Everything was about his schedule and sex was not a part of his schedule.

After a short four months together, Jeremy and I went to a luau-themed work party of mine. It was our first social event together and it didn't go well. It went so badly that I swore I would never go with him to a party again. He did wear a Hawaiian shirt, which was nice, but when we got to the party, after a few short introductions, he sat down on the edge of a picnic bench, made no effort to talk to anybody and took out his phone and played games on it. I was so confused by this behavior. At least he could talk to me, but he didn't even do that. Everyone noticed and I felt very embarrassed.

The one moment that he did finally mingle a little was when my co-worker friend and host of the party went over to talk to him. Afterwards, she came to me and said that he didn't respond and walked away, and he said something odd too, so she felt she had to come to me and ask what was going on with him. I asked Jeremy if something was wrong and told him what my friend had said. He denied that he did anything weird. I told him—as frustration built in me—that she would have no reason to lie and simply wanted to know if there was something wrong, since he'd walked away from her while she was talking to him. He would not answer me. I told him that we needed to leave. I was beyond upset with him at this point. During the drive home, I let Jeremy know that I was only asking a question and not accusing him of anything, because he was behaving as though my enquiry was more like an attack on him. He took it way out of proportion.

Because I didn't understand autistic behavior at the time, this incident really disturbed me, and it was only the first of many eye-openers for me that he was indeed different and difficult. The red flags became more and more visible and uncomfortable as time went on in our relationship. But I guess I was in too deep and I wanted to be married. The good qualities still overshadowed the strange behavior and with having low self-esteem myself, on top of not understanding autistic behavior, I felt I was doing something wrong or not understanding him and so on.

Right before he proposed, we made a short visit to my parents' home. My sister was playing on a basketball team and the whole family went to her game. Jeremy had never seen a live team sport before and only had an idea of it from watching sports television.

We arrived at a tiny gym and my sister and her team were on the other side of the court from where we were sitting. Jeremy was the loudest person in the whole place. He screamed; not just rooting for them but giving direction as well during the whole game, like he was a head coach. I was so embarrassed. I mentioned to him that he was loud, and he said, "Oh, they needed a coach and they really loved it." He couldn't compute his inappropriateness. I could tell on my dad's face that he too was puzzled by Jeremy, but he said to me in kindness that, well, "Jeremy was really involved."

We got married and a few years went by; I worked hard on my career, but we moved a lot because of his military duties. Life was busy having to reestablish my jobs so there wasn't a lot of time to stay mad or argue with him. Although I wasn't happy, I was also glad to be married and have a routine. It was difficult to imagine leaving him and dating again so I stuck it out. I also kept in mind that maybe he was only different due to his upbringing and losses in life. His brother died when he was ten years old and his parents were missionaries. They traveled and home-schooled him. He was very sheltered from the outside world.

When we started a family was when I began to do more research into his behaviors and stumbled upon Asperger's Syndrome. All the boxes were checked. He was clearly autistic and very high functioning [River's note: many people now prefer the terms 'low needs' and 'high needs', officially known as autism levels 1, 2, and 3].

Figuring out ways to talk with him more effectively helped during arguments and he would make some changes for a little while, but he always fell back into his kind of hard-wired thinking and actions. He suffers from OCD behaviors which fall into the autistic spectrum; awkwardness, self-absorption and schedules are his hard-wiring. His very black-and-white thinking is often difficult. Black-and-white thinking is just that. He does something a certain way and that is how it stays. No matter if it might hurt others. There is no reciprocity or understanding that there is gray in everything.

In my training as a marriage and family counselor, negotiation and compromise are much of the foundation that makes a good marriage and relationship work. It is certainly a brain twister sometimes when I understand how marriage works, and yet my own is like an entirely different way of being with someone.

I want to tell you one last thing. In Jeremy's element he does great. He is well respected at work. This is the one thing that makes it such a secret. When he gets home, the mask comes off and he crashes. And this is typical behavior in a lot of people, right? However, the fun Jeremy is also the mask. He can rarely be serious unless he is telling people what to do. And if he doesn't like someone, the mask is off, and he lets that person know he dislikes them. No butt-kissing. The awkwardness comes out when he is upset with someone or something that does not fit his schedule because people with autism usually have poor emotional regulation. Work is usually a task to be done so the lack of emotional regulation can be hidden well in a military situation. Add in an emotion and you may see the mask come off, and the real person underneath who is awkward and unstable.

In conclusion, I've learned that one way to have a better life with my autistic hubby is to tell him exactly how I'm feeling in a very calm manner. Even though my feelings may be strong, and I want to scream, I know that if my voice is raised or I come off as abrasive in any way, he will completely shut down and not hear a word that I'm saying.

One time I told him, in a calm and gentle voice, that I was losing respect for him because of how he was treating me.

He said, "That's not good."

It was the first time I received a response that wasn't a comment putting things back onto me. Such as his usual "That's not my problem" attitude. It was very nice to hear him respond and I felt heard. However, I will also say this. He heard me, yes, but quickly forgot the conversation the next day. This is common, and I understand now that their processing is different, and they need time for things to sink in when it has to do with a person outside of themselves. **It's so hard for them to be in someone else's shoes.** So, I know that I must keep strong and tell him again, maybe several times and in a calm voice. I try to remind him in the moment; if he says something unkind, I let him know right away. It's work. It's not easy. I falter sometimes because I'm human. I've also learned to be easier on myself if I do blow up at him, because at the end of the day, I need to take care of me.

* * *

River's comments:

THE SAME AS how Amanda met her hubby, I also met Gil through a dating site, eHarmony. Those dating sites really enable people to wear a good mask. I remember a picture of Gil that I really liked that showed him at a rescue zoo. I thought he might love animals, which was attractive to me. And he really does love animals. Dating sites show all the good stuff.

I must add how ironic it felt that Gil also has two dogs that he never got trained and that he refuses to get trained. They do have a wild side to them, and I understand his reasoning. However, after I talked to a professional dog trainer about his dogs and heard they could be trained and do well, Gil still refused.

I can completely relate to the low self-esteem aspect of Amanda's story. I too was super down on my luck with a very low self-image and self-esteem. I wanted someone to take charge and Gil did that. He was the whole package for me. As Amanda alluded to, I simply wanted to be married and didn't care much about a big romance. Security was key for me. Little did we both know what was in store.

I am continually amazed by the similarities in all our stories. I too loved how Gil didn't smother me. He let me completely be myself and one thing that was nice was that he didn't ask a lot of questions such as: "Where were you?" or "Where are you going?" or "Why do you feel that way when you should feel this way?" Or, the biggest pet peeve for me, "You need to do it that way."

He didn't mind if I said something weird or laughed from nervousness. He didn't notice my embarrassing moments. In fact, and I didn't know it at the time, he didn't notice my facial expressions at all, or the awkwardness that I felt at the time, because, well, of course he was autistic. From my experience and from what I have read time and again, autistic folks can't notice those things, and they are so focused on their next move to make sure the other person sticks around, that is all that matters.

How do they do this without all the social cues? According to what one reads online, it is mostly by mirroring. And from my experience in hearing from wives of autistic men and how they were whisked off their feet, it seems the autistic men go big or go home. There are red flags, like Amanda mentioned, but the other aspects can be intoxicating. The humor and vulnerability and awkwardness are endearing because many are smart, with a strong need to be needed by you. I really needed to be needed.

Many autistic men are successful in business because of this mirroring trait, and they can use it very well to attract you to them but when it comes down to it, and the getting-to-know-each-other phase is over, you are either too far in to do anything about it or the feeling of being crazy starts to kick in. They think so differently that our brains start to 'break' a little bit from trying to understand their communication and/or lack thereof.

Amanda told us about her husband's five dogs and how he happened to never mention all the dogs until it was time for her to move in. A neurotypical person might think that he tried to hide them from her for fear she would not agree to move in, let's say. But truthfully, it may never have occurred to him that she'd need to know. I can't speak for him of course, but he may think that because he feeds them and they are his, what's the big deal, and why is she upset that I didn't tell her about the dogs? I understand this completely. There has been many a time that I find out something at the last minute and then I can't do anything about it.

For me, the issue is often an event that comes directly to Gil and not to me because—and I will get back to this later—Gil never talks to his family about me; he barely talks to them at all. This means that he doesn't let me know if a wedding is coming up, or a trip with his brother, or a trip by himself, or any of those events that I should know about. When he tells me last minute, I get so upset and appear, to him, like a needy and crazy person. So, I understand that lack of information. What I have done to help with this is to ask him questions at least once a week. Simple questions like: Any family or business events being planned? Are you planning on going anywhere in the next two weeks? This helps eliminate a lot of last-minute issues and heartache I feel when I'm not included in his world, unless he is asked by the party inviting him to tell me about the event. He must be *told* to tell me. And I can't tell him to tell me once and have him remember that. **I must ask the questions every week.**

Amanda told me that Jeremy would send flowers or do things for her that he was *told* to do. Again, they really need to be told, but they usually will not listen or hear the person telling them to do something unless they deeply respect that person or are conditioned to listen to them. Gil, I have seen, will do whatever his brother says to do, no matter what. Jeremy listened to his mom, who said to send Amanda flowers, so he did.

This is a tough one for neurotypical partners. From my experience with Gil, I can say it takes a lot for him to be conditioned to listen to someone new in his life; it usually won't happen unless he has no one else. He picks only a few people to completely trust and sadly, the new wife or girlfriend will be last on the list of full trust. Honestly, it took many years for him to trust me as his long-term person and even still, he will not fully trust me. It hurts, but I accept it. This is not always true but sometimes, due to negativity about, say, marriage, they may absorb messages such as: The wife is not to be trusted. She will divorce you and take your money. A wife or partner can walk away, and cause hurt. A family member is always there.

Schedules and gaming are classic issues that are known to be common in autistic people. We all love games but when it becomes their 'special interest' there is no stopping them. Stimming is often talked about with autism as a form of self-soothing. Some may do rapid hand motions or discuss one topic over and over. It is clearer in high-needs autism. In lower-needs, or level 1 autism, it is less clear.

I still look for signs that Gil might be addicted to something and focused on one thing, but he doesn't do that. He has some rapid mood changes if his schedule is changed but that is really all he does. He has a strict schedule in the mornings before work. I can tell you everything he does each morning because it never changes. At first, I really liked this because I get scattered in the mornings and he has kept me to a regular sleep schedule, which makes me more productive. So, there is always good in schedules. And Gil also handles schedule changes well, if they are not drastic, but I know it really is hard for him to get back on track so schedules are important, and strict routines for one person are difficult to live with. If I was strict about my own schedule, we would never see each other. I conform to his schedule a lot so I can be near him and feel a connection that way.

And speaking of connection, I've often heard that it's common for autistic people to not be very sex driven. Some, with high libidos, do like sex but for the most part it's put into a schedule. The romance part makes no sense at all to most autistic people.

Amanda's example of her husband's need for gaming over sex or connection with his new love is typical. A neurotypical person may have sex or use romance to get close to another person. Even if their libido may be low, they will continue to find connection with another person physically or romantically or both. For a person on the spectrum, touching is often difficult and uncomfortable. Many would rather not touch but that doesn't mean that they don't want to connect.

Amanda and I have talked about this. The often-heard opinion that people on the autistic spectrum don't want to connect to other people is not true. They want connection one hundred percent but very often, only know how to give fifteen percent. So, when Amanda or I feel frustrated with our men because they won't connect with us physically or romantically, using loud words and frustration only makes things worse for us and for them. We instead need to tell them to hug us or to watch a TV show with us or play a game with us. They will not initiate it most of the time, but doing those things is a way to connect for them. Again, not easy for us but reality is key. Understanding is key. Patience is key in a neurodiverse relationship.

Lastly, Amanda and I have both noticed that being in the military is generally a good fit for an autistic person. The compartmentalizing and great focus on the task at hand is easy for them. Amanda mentioned that her husband is most comfortable in telling people what to do. Certainly the military offers direct rules and guidelines to follow, which is ideal for an autistic person. As for Gil, his career is similar in that it deals with numbers and figures and facts, more so than socializing and building relationships with people.

FROM LOSS AND GRIEF TO

BEWILDERMENT AND

ACCEPTANCE

MY (RIVER'S) STORY

RECENTLY, I WAS OUT DRIVING WITH GIL, my partner or as I sometimes call him, my forever fiancé. We like to do small road trips for the day. Gil put on some music, a playlist of songs he felt that I would like. And he was right. I liked them. But I couldn't sing along to them, not aloud, and found myself feeling a deep sense of sadness. He was finally playing songs that I liked. Not songs that only he liked. We had hit another milestone. It was wonderful, although I felt miserable.

I asked him, "Gil, did you pick those songs for me?"

He said, "Yes."

"Thank you."

He said, "Well, I was listening to them all day yesterday, so I like them."

I said nothing. I chuckled a bit to myself and

59

then I began to cry softly as I looked out the window at the brilliant clouds. A breathtaking day in southern California. Gil is never able to really say that he did something for me. He knew he did, and in his heart he did, but his words said otherwise. 'All about him' rings in my head, yet I know better. This is how he connects with me the best that he can. His words take on a different meaning in his head from how they sound to the 'regular' world of us neurotypicals.

I reminded myself in that moment: *It's constant. I know he is who he is. I have accepted my life with him and how it will be. I chose wisely and, my gosh I even wrote a book about it.*

With life's twists and turns, there will always be those moments. I am aware and I accept it, but oh, how much I really wanted to sing to those songs.

I said to him, "I do love the songs but it's making me nuts not being able to sing to them."

He quickly responded, "Oh PLEASE!! Please don't sing! Don't be like your Aunt Jane."

My gut clenched. He hit a nerve mentioning Aunt Jane. When Gil and I went on our first road trip, ten years ago, he told me not to sing in the car. I sheepishly said, "Okay." And proceeded to apologize and mention my aunt who also would sing in the car, and how sometimes it got to be a little much. But I was no Aunt Jane. I would softly sing to myself to a song I loved. But after him telling me not to, I never sang in front of him again. Not even in the house could I hum or sing even a tiny bit in his hearing range.

I stopped singing altogether until recently, after beginning my life in a new light, rebuilding and finding friendships outside of our home to fulfil those emotional needs that Gil simply cannot fill. I spent years and years of struggle before he was diagnosed with autism. Those years were incredibly difficult and now, little by little, even though my Gil is stubborn, we reach milestones like songs I like on a road trip. And maybe, just maybe, he and I can negotiate that I sing a couple songs on our trips in the future. There is always a chance I may not be able to do that with him. I accept that fact.

I changed my tone and said—in a halfhearted way so he wouldn't feel like I was lashing out at him—"Oh man, I just can't do it. What else can we listen to? You have audio books or something?"

He didn't get mad. He simply changed the song list to a middle ground group of songs. Another big milestone!

I also loved and wanted to sing to those songs as well, but I let that go too. I let it rest. He was really trying. I think for the next road trip, I'll tell him we need an audio book that he likes.

As I write those last few lines, I hear his car drive up with his radio turned loud to the songs that I like. I have to stop typing. I put my hands on my face and sit still for a while. For ten years, he never ever would listen to my songs and now he listens to them of his own accord. It's baffling. But is it? He's thinking of me. He copies so well. What does *he* like? I wonder if he even knows or if it is important to him. He goes with what others like if he is trying to get them into his life. It's his way of connecting. He is connecting to me through song right now. It's special. However, I'm not there within his connection. It can really baffle a neurotypical's brain.

I'm a person in his life that he relies on, and he wants desperately for me to feel comfortable in his world, yet he can't connect to me in the ways that make me feel connected to someone. Yet, he is happy when I am happy with something that he did. It is desperately difficult when I step outside the day-to-day stuff and realize that he will never truly understand me. He will only get the depth of what he thinks of me from his perspective. And I know it is a spectrum. It's not the same for everyone. For Gil and me, this is how it is.

Why is this such a big thing? So, he doesn't like my songs, or I guess now he does, after nine years of him telling me he hated them. After nine years of never ever being able to hum in the house or belt out a tune as I love doing so much.

I'm reminded of a Christmas before I knew he was autistic, when I lost myself in the moment of Christmas morning, looking at my tree. I began to sing a Christmas carol and he shouted at me to shut up. I was so upset; I tore down the tree right then on Christmas morning. At a time that had always been my favorite, I found myself in a big house with a man who hated Christmas songs, hated if I sang a single tune in front of him, and told me time and again that Christmas is just a day off work.

After therapy and his diagnosis only three years ago, things have been better. That road trip was a huge milestone for us. Although things remain difficult, I am not angry anymore. I don't yell or cry on the floor, wondering what I am doing to make him so awful to me. I will feel sad at times, and irked, and of course may have a full-blown blowup with him, but nothing like it was before I knew of his autism. His way is who he is. If he tries—and I see him trying more and more—that is all I ask for. It's truly a gift to know it's not all me. He is autistic. He was misunderstood all his life. He reacts to survive. And he does love me very deeply in his own way. I can't ask for more than that.

When I met Gil, I was not my best self. In fact, I was a complete disaster. Life had gotten extremely difficult within a matter of only a few years. My mom died, my dad was seriously ill, my marriage failed after fifteen years, I lost several homes during the crash of '08, lost a business my husband and I ran for ten years, several extended family members and friends died, and several pets died as well. My once picket-fence life was torn down, piece by piece. 'You don't know what you have until it's gone' took root in me at a whole new level.

Within that time, I cared for both of my sick parents for five years, which led to a tumultuous relationship with extended family members. Misunderstandings and gossip abounded, and my dad's altered mental state did not help. There is never right or wrong when caring for a loved one. There is only doing your best with what you've got. But at the time, I allowed all of it to tear me down.

I feel the need to explain why the next journey in my life, after losing everything so suddenly, led me to someone like Gil. I reached out to family, only to get shut down and shut out. I love my family very much. But I was left abandoned, knocked down and misunderstood due to events that took place with no one at fault. Simply, life struck like a tornado that neither I nor my family were prepared for. Picking up the pieces and caring for my dad the best that I could, led to lots of gossip that I wasn't doing it right or I wasn't caring for him as I should be. Out of all the loss, the greatest loss was rejection and abandonment by my family. It was no wonder that I would choose a man like Gil, because he felt normal to me. He ignored my feelings. He misunderstood my words. I felt that was all I deserved. I almost relished the put-downs and exaggerated outbursts if I did something he was uncomfortable with, like chewing too loud, humming to myself, or talking too much.

Being an only child, never able to have children and now no family except for my dying dad, dropped me into loneliness and grief. Not a good mixture. I began dating quickly to find a husband again to save me from the loneliness. I wanted to be swept up and cared for. I fell hard for a man that only wanted a good time. That loss sent me over the edge.

I considered ending my life but remembered when my dad's brother took his own life and the pain it brought to my dad and the family. I couldn't do that to them. I was homeless, hungry, abandoned. What could I do to keep going?

A trusted friend advised me to go back to school, so I did. I received a grant for telling my story and worked as a student worker. I continued to want to find a man to spend the rest of my life with, and when I met Gil online, I hoped that he could be someone that would allow me to catch my breath. That I could slow down and relax with him. To feel safe and cared for because I had no energy to fight with the world anymore.

However, our first date didn't go very well. We met at a restaurant for dinner. I arrived early, as I normally do, to calm myself a bit before he got there, and he arrived on the dot at 6:00 PM. I was sitting in the waiting area to get a table and when he came in, he looked at me and smiled a quirky, cute half smile. He was about the same height as me. He wore loose-fitting jeans and a button-up dark blue and black striped shirt. I noticed his brilliant blue eyes had a twinkle in them. He was clean-shaven and didn't look his age at all. Although his profile said he was ten years my elder, he looked my age, or even younger than me. He seemed simply adorable to me right away. And like someone I could be myself around. I can still remember how relaxed I felt as soon as I saw him.

As he walked towards me, a lady came over and told me that I looked so much like Sheryl Crow that she had to come up and say something to me. Sheryl was in town at the time and the lady, for a moment, thought I was her. What an ego boost that was for me! Felt great! Gil's first words to me were, "Who was that?"

I said, "Just a random person saying I looked like Sheryl Crow."

Gil asked, "Who is Sheryl Crow?"

I looked at him, puzzled and thinking he was joking, but he didn't know who she was. I told him that she was a famous singer. He shrugged in an awkward way and didn't seem to care. He said, "Oh okay then." The boost of confidence I felt faded into a kind of strange discomfort as I lost the easy feeling after he opened his mouth. I let him know that I'd given our names to the hostess and there would be about a ten-minute wait.

We sat side by side in silence, but the feeling of comfort flooded inside me again. I felt at home with him in the silence. We were soon seated. Within ten minutes after ordering cocktails and saying the usual, nice place, how are you and glad to meet you, he told me that he had dated a woman significantly younger than him, and that they had broken up a few months ago. Not a very wise introduction for himself. I didn't think *how odd* as I would now, so I responded with an 'okay, cool' expression. An "oh, uh huh" as I sipped my cocktail.

We ordered hamburgers, ate, and made small talk. After dinner, I excused myself to the restroom and upon my return to the table, before I even sat down, he said, "I've got to go." The date was over so suddenly, like he wanted out of there. I was having fun, but I thought, *oh well, story of my life*. The dinner was done. He had paid already, and we walked out together to his car.

He said, "Sorry, I really got to go right now. I'm meeting my ex to give her something that I forgot to give to her."

I shrugged and said, "Okay. Well goodbye then." And we parted ways.

I walked to my car feeling very understandably uncomfortable. Why would he really tell me what he was doing? I guess he didn't care much about hurting my feelings. *There went the best and worst date since I joined eHarmony*. To feel better, I went directly to my computer to find someone else.

Three days went by, and two dates later with other people, I decided to see one of them exclusively. Then I got a text from Gil. It read something like "I enjoyed our date. Would you like to go out again?"

I texted him back and said, "I'm so sorry. I think I've found someone."

Gil continued to text me anyway and honestly, I liked the attention and I thought Gil and I could at least be friends. I felt so comfortable texting him any old thing I wanted and having him reply kindly to me. He would answer all my texts. That wasn't a normal thing for me. It felt nice. And his texts had some long words in them that I had to look up before responding, which was kind of fun. Made me feel smart.

In October of 2010, about a month after I'd met

Gil, on Halloween night, things began to get weird with the new guy. I went to a party by myself. Feeling lonely without a date, I left the party early and spent Halloween night alone. I also spent Thanksgiving alone, all the while texting Gil what was going on with me, and his texts back were so sweet. He would say things like he understood how I felt. He felt the same way about the holidays and how hard it was to be alone. I felt a connection with him through the texting. We became friends over texts.

I continued to try to make it work with the other guy until after the holidays when he took off to Oregon and began to ignore my calls. Within a few weeks, that relationship was over, and I gave Gil a call. As friends, Gil and I met at the same restaurant as before and got tipsy together. During the dinner, I will always remember his face looking dead-on at me, like he could see into my soul, as he asked with a tone of excitement, "Wanna go to my place?"

I responded questioningly, "Well, are you sure?"

He said, again looking straight into my eyes, "Why not?"

Mesmerized and tipsy, I murmured a shy, "Okay."

I followed him to his house. He was so funny and fun and awkward that it relaxed me as I fell into his arms and into sex like we were old lovers.

A few weeks after we started dating, I fell ill with a lung infection and Gil let me stay in his house. He checked on me during his lunch breaks and brought me soup. This kindness caused my heart to melt.

After three months of dating, he flew us to Cancun for five days where we stayed in a luxurious hotel. It was my birthday and he asked the staff to surprise me with a cake! It was SO glorious!! I remember sitting on the balcony of our room looking out at the ocean and thinking of my mom. I cried and cried. I finally had a moment to grieve. My inner voice told her that I was going to be okay. I told her how beautiful the ocean was. She loved the ocean more than anything. I told her that after all the pain and loss, that I had found the love of my life and I was going to be okay.

After the Cancun trip, I only saw Gil on the weekends because of his busy work schedule, and those weekends were filled with fine dining and lots of drinking. At times during our nights out, he would say things that hurt my feelings, but Sunday morning all was forgotten. We would go hiking or take a drive to the mountains or to the beach. It was glorious fun.

Although our Saturday nights often ended with uncomfortable words and feelings, I continued to ignore those times because he, for the most part, let me be me. He didn't ask much of me. Didn't ask many questions about my past. When I talked to him, I felt he was listening and not judging me by his silence.

Very often he would say something rude to me, or about others, and it rolled over me because I had been so beaten down. I felt mad at the world, as he did. And when beaten down by life, it's easy to go negative and carry a chip on your shoulder or play the victim.

But within a few short months, as Gil and I got closer, deeper and more destructive struggles began between us. Life remained a crazy whirlwind of events, even though I thought I had met a man that could help me pick up the pieces and start fresh.

Ironically, Gil's parents fell ill only six months after we met, and he became their caregiver before both died. I had a lot of experience in caregiving and thought it very rude when Gil called his ex from years past for advice on caregiving. I remember being in tears that Gil didn't come to me first. I felt I was meant to be in Gil's life at that time to help him since I had so much experience in that area.

I took a lot to heart with Gil at that time. I was so beaten up mentally from everything I'd gone through that I even blamed myself when Gil's mom passed. She had fallen and I kicked myself that I couldn't do more to prevent that from happening.

Gil and I had several breakups for short periods of time and then we'd end up back together again, to start the chaos over. It wasn't until I moved in with Gil, after four years of tumultuous dating, that I felt we were truly together.

When we finally took the leap, it was under extreme conditions. Soon after his mom passed, he had broken up with me for longer than ever before. He'd talked about going to Vietnam and Thailand, two places I had long dreamed of going to, and after the breakup he took the trip that he and I had planned together with his brother instead. I truly felt that he had broken up with me right before the trip in order to be a free man and have a good time with his brother. I found out later that wasn't the case at all. He had completely forgotten that he had talked to me about us both going, and I believe him (I've since learned that this isn't unusual for some autistic people). But all the same, I was devastated. I dated someone else within that three-month period, but he was not Gil. I missed Gil very much.

When Gil returned from his trip, he wanted me back. I told him that first I would have to move in with him, that we were to get married in Thailand and go to counseling. He said okay to all three. I broke up with the man I had been seeing and Gil and I went to counseling; I moved into his house and began to make wedding plans. I talked with a good friend I had met during my time at a Buddhist monastery, who lived in Thailand at the time and who could officiate.

But wedding plans were put on hold when my dad died. My last words to my dad were, "Gil and I are going to get married. I'm going to be okay." I'll never forget his sweet and gentle smile back at me, with a bit of surprise and then assurance that he knew I was going to be okay. He was a traditional old-school dad. He worried about me not finding someone again. An emotional storm lifted in me after my dad died. He had suffered for so long. That feeling of relief mixed with grief is a kind of sadness that one can only understand if they experience it. I was tired and felt completely alone in the world. I felt Gil was all I had.

Within five weeks following my dad's death, Gil's dad died. We were both now adult orphans.

I mentioned to Gil that we needed a fresh start. Wedding plans turned into house hunting. Within six months we moved into the home of my dreams. It was the most incredible home I'd ever imagined myself living in! The neighborhood was beautiful. A dream come true.

Only a few months after our move, Gil's brother invited him to Costa Rica. Gil, matter-of-factly, told me he was going with him. Only him and his brother. I was shocked! Our next trip was supposed to be for our wedding.

It took a lot of convincing, but Gil finally agreed that I come along and that we have a ceremony in Costa Rica. A small one sounded great. His brother and a cousin of mine who lived there would be our witnesses. And yes, I happened to have a friend in Thailand and now, a distant relative in Costa Rica. Those fortuitous circumstances gave me strong vibes of it being 'meant to be' each time.

I began to make plans with a coordinator in Costa Rica. Three weeks of planning flew by, and while we were driving to the store one day, Gil got a call from his brother telling him that we would meet him in a different area.

Gil said, "Okay." Completely forgetting that I made plans for our ceremony in the city I thought we were going to. I was so upset that I told Gil not to go! This was too painful. I felt that I looked like the terribly controlling fiancée to his family, whom I hardly knew. They were never informed that we were, or I was, planning a wedding. Gill stayed home because I put my foot down and we were able to get more settled into our new home.

I fell into the pattern of living with him and wedding plans became non-existent. Counseling didn't help us. He wouldn't do the exercises that he was asked to do. I felt it was always me being too sensitive or too needy. We continued to have more weekend nights ending in fights. Sometimes awful fights with me sobbing on the floor as he stood there saying and doing nothing.

This continual frustration lasted for almost two more years. And although we were living together, I began to feel very alone, and like we were only dating again. The schedule of going out on Saturday nights stayed the same. During the week, we would usually have dinner together but we never talked. He said he was too tired. I tried to arrange things so we'd have time together to talk about our day for even a few minutes during the week, but this seemed too much for him, and trying to force him left him sitting in silence as I talked with no responses from him.

Feeling alone, I joined groups such as toastmasters and grief groups. But the evening meetings would often end late and I would wake him when I got home, which was a big deal. I dove into home repairs and changes to make the new house of my dreams into a home. This kept my mind busy. It was exciting to create beautiful spaces, but that's when I found out that making changes was not ideal for Gil. He would come home from work only to get frustrated that I had moved things around. He would not only get frustrated; he would get angry.

I began, for my emotional survival, to become a bit numb to Gil's harsh words at times, and to our extreme misunderstandings. I talked to him about marriage several times only for him to blow me off, now saying that he would never get married to anyone. I gave up at some point and asked him to at least have a commitment ceremony, so I could feel like I belonged to him and his family, and to have a party to get to know his side of the family. This was still a no. He didn't want to visit family much. I was lonely and felt isolated.

Then, out of the blue, Gil told me he was going to Nepal . . . by himself. Of course, that's when I decided I had had enough! I was not going to feel isolated and invisible anymore. While he was gone, I looked for answers and that is when autism provided the missing pieces of the puzzle.

I made him promise that when he got home, that we would have our commitment ceremony. He promised that we would. I am still waiting for a commitment ceremony.

Since then, Gil and I have moved once again because that big, beautiful house of my dreams was not right for us. My dreams are a distant memory now. Now is all about making decisions on my own as to how my life will go with Gil. Now is writing this book in order to help others. Now is for me, and being strong and making wise decisions. No more self-destruction. Learning of his autism shattered the horrible, trapped pattern that I was in. I had jumped from one frying pan—my life before Gil—into another, even hotter one. Now the flames are low and life is better. Not great. But much better.

A man who is autistic, like Gil, can be extremely good at wearing a kind of 'mask' in the beginning. Not to fool or take advantage of people, but simply to cover up what he has learned about himself that doesn't work while dating. He can be awkward but it's endearing. Most will have a laser-beam focus, like no other, and it's intoxicating when we are their focus. They absolutely do not wear the mask with ill intent to get us to their lair and then eat us alive. No. They simply want us so much so that they do whatever it takes. They live in the moment of what's needed right now. And of course, we all put on a mask in the beginning when we want someone to like us. But oh my, in my experience, they do it much more intensely.

Dating is the easy part too, because it's more about doing things than getting down to the nitty-gritty of making decisions for and with another person. The honeymoon period drops off so abruptly because home is where you get down to the reality of life, where it hits you in the face. And when you get to their lair, all masks come off and you're left asking nothing but what the . . .?

I still love Gil madly and dearly even though he is not a noble knight anymore who saved me from the awful of my life when we met. His shining armor is cracked and rusted, and his magnificent white horse has died.

If I had known then what I know now, a lot of

heartache would have been avoided. However, if I had known he was autistic from the beginning, I don't know if I would have taken a book and read all about it. And I probably wouldn't have found a book like this one that shared the side of the wife/partner and all that she endures including the good, the bad and the ugly.

There are many groups on Facebook for us ladies, with thousands upon thousands of women talking about their difficult lives with their autistic man. Our common experiences leap out at us: Loneliness, despite being in a relationship. Feeling that no one on the 'outside' can understand. And the fact that our entire lives, in every aspect, revolve around our autistic partners. They're very, very, VERY high-maintenance partners.

We have our funny moments as well, in these groups. There are women who know that their man is autistic and ask for guidance. Many are still in the honeymoon phase that is so darn intoxicating. There are those freshly coming off of that phase and although it's not easy, some say that they would do it all over again. Their autistic man is worth it! Would I do it all over again? No. I obviously was in a bad place in my life when I met Gil. I try not to look back and I appreciate my life with him, but I wouldn't do it all over again. To be brutally honest, and I know Gil would want me to be, I would run fast and far away.

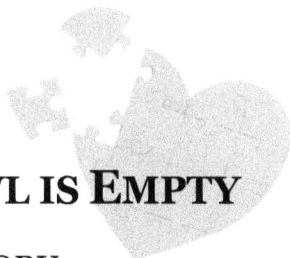

THE WATER BOWL IS EMPTY

APRIL'S STORY

MY HUSBAND JOHN AND I HAVE been together for almost eight years now and have been married for over six of those. Sometimes I count the duration of time to the week. It hasn't been easy, nor horrific, but over half of the time, it's been difficult. I love John dearly, and he loves me, which is what keeps us working on our marriage no matter how hard it gets.

Within a period of two and a half years, John and I went through tragic losses together. His mom passed away, then one of my cousins passed away. Shortly after my cousin's death, my mom passed away, and then one of my sisters five months after. And then only a few months after those awful losses, just when I felt I could begin to pick up the pieces, our beloved dog died and another one of my sisters passed away. How does one recover from so much loss in such a short period of time? But I made it through with the help of my husband. He was my rock most of the time. He sometimes jumped into control mode, as in having to handle everything on his own and take care of a few things that didn't need his attention during that difficult time, but he also took care of tasks that were too hard for me to do while I was immersed in my grief.

Luckily, since our marriage, we have experienced good times together too, such as my son Devon's graduation from high school, and a couple of trips to Hawaii and Lake Tahoe.

During the early stages of our courtship and marriage, I took John to be simply a little different than other men, but glossed over his controlling side. We had experienced so much loss; I knew that people act differently when grieving so I chalked some of his control issues up to his way of grieving his mom's death, and also to having to deal with me and my grieving on top of that. But as time went on, I realized that something was not right with him. I had feelings of wanting to leave him but felt perplexed as to why he acted the way he did. I thought I might be too sensitive, or that it was the result of *my* issues.

I knew I loved him, and the thought of divorce was terrible for me, so I decided to seek professional counseling. During a session with my psychologist in the summer of 2018, I described arguments, tiffs, and disagreements so that I could find ways to 'be the bigger person' or just get through them without losing my mind and wanting to leave my husband. I mentioned that vacations were nice, and we got along during trips away, but daily life events were getting harder and harder. The magic of the vacations never lasted long enough to get us through our problems.

After I mentioned these struggles to my

psychologist, who had thirty years' experience I might add, he said, "Is there any way John could be on the autism spectrum?"

I responded a quick "YES!" And then I felt a yank at my guts as to why I couldn't see it right away. My son from another marriage has high functioning autism. How could I have not seen it in my new husband? This shocked me, to say the least. But I then started to connect the dots and oh yes, John had to be on the spectrum. That explained so much. It was a breath of fresh air to finally have something to go on, but I also felt my heart sink to the floor. Hard to explain all the emotions I felt and difficult for me to not kick myself for not seeing it sooner.

While keeping client privacy intact, my psychologist told me a story about a client who had a significant other with very similar actions to John and who did have an autism diagnosis. He explained how his client was frustrated and needed tips on communication with her husband for the sake of their relationship.

I had only five sessions with my psychologist. We had a few laughs about the absurdity of some situations within my relationship and he gave me some tips, but it didn't take away the extreme, daily frustration I still felt.

Learning some communication skills helped a little bit, but John would take my comments and discussions as if I was 'bossing him'. He would say, "Okay Mother." For example, I once pointed out that the dog bowl was low on water. I told him this while I was lying down with ice on my shoulder after physical therapy. He said that he constantly thinks I am bossing him around and being demanding. I simply told him the bowl was getting empty and I was down on the couch thinking he might notice and simply fill the bowl with water, because I needed to rest and keep my shoulder still and on ice. But filling the bowl was not the issue anymore. The simple comment led into an attitude of me 'bossing' him around again and he begrudgingly filled the bowl. He turned something so simple into a big deal.

The 'bossing' is only one thing of many that makes life difficult with John. Lately I have been wondering if I've been gaslighted. Gaslighting is a term used by psychologists to describe abusive behavior mostly acted out by narcissistic and manipulative people. It is a way to belittle someone and make them think *they* are the problem or 'crazy' when they are not. But I can tell that John doesn't consciously try to convince me I am crazy. He simply does whatever he can to get out of a difficult talk or situation. We do have bad disagreements, but when we practice kindness (as I call it), we *are* able to talk through our difficulties. Kindness includes such things as me reminding him that I am not attacking him, but only speaking to him to resolve a problem, or talk about something we need for the home or family etc.

He has told me that he has trouble expressing himself. And I am very happy that he recognizes this in himself. He does have trouble admitting his part in our communication problems, but I remind myself that it is not me, and only his inability to understand some issues that come up in relationships. He hasn't been able to identify or label what his difficulty is, but it has gotten much better just from his realization that he struggles. And sometimes I truly must remind myself that he struggles and keep a good sense of humor within it all. I'll never forget one time he said, "I'm sorry . . . that *you made* me say that to you."

Another sign of autism that I noticed in John was when he had a meltdown over the remote control for the bedroom TV. I could feel his anxiety seething off him while I channel surfed.

He said, with a frustrated tone, "You are taking forever!" I strongly and deliberately had to remind him that it was my turn for the TV and that he needs to share. Sounded like I was talking to a five-year-old.

I even asked him recently, "Are you five?!" due to a breakdown in communication. We go through communication problems almost daily even though we talk about how we feel around the situation.

John has not been properly diagnosed but his behavior points very much to autism, especially in the common area of not understanding his emotions or others' emotions. So, he understandably cannot read what others are feeling and what their emotions mean. He has agreed with me on this. I must explain it very clearly and provide a very detailed scenario for him to understand. This goes back to me feeling that I must talk to him like he is a child. It's not easy because he is an adult, and my husband and partner.

For example, he's had a horrible time adjusting to being a stepdad to my son. Devon was fifteen when we got married. Devon is very sweet and can be easily rattled if he can't express himself clearly. This is one of his challenges due to autism.

I had to say to John, "What if you had a fifteen-year-old daughter when we got married and she didn't want me to be involved with her? I would respect her wishes and back off. I would understand that it would take time and patience for her to let me into her world. She doesn't know me, and I don't know her."

My point is that I had to explain the very basics of a new stepfamily relationship. It doesn't come naturally for him. He has no insight or instinct for new family relationships. He also wants to parent in the 1950s style that his mom and dad used with him. I've had to explain that parenting has changed over the decades. He has a kind of locked-in attitude on copying what his parents did. This does make sense, due to his inability to read social cues and adjust to how times have changed, but even understanding it doesn't help me in moments when I want to pull my hair out and can't muster up the words to explain to him issues that are common sense to me.

And allow me to jump into talking about his strict schedule. For the living room TV, he wants me to abide by a certain program or movie viewing schedule. He gets up early, goes to a coffee shop, comes home, goes back to bed. He has insomnia, which is a common issue for people on the spectrum as well. He has been put on anti-depressants and anti-anxiety meds to help him sleep. He gets happier while on them and gets more sleep and then announces that he is going to stop taking them because they make him feel weird. When he is happy, hope wells up in me that he will be better, only for me to feel a letdown when he stops his meds. Why do I keep hoping?

Also, he lives in the past, watching WWII movies endlessly. But what is most debilitating is his inability to heal from the grief of losing both of his parents. He pines over them, constantly stuck with his loss. His dad died when he was sixteen and this understandably traumatized him, but he relives it sometimes as if it happened yesterday. Also, several times a year, he posts on Facebook how much he misses his mom. I'm glad he had a connection with them of course, but I see it as disabling if you are in bed most of the time, still holding onto the grief. I am at my wits' end because he won't stay on helpful meds or get professional help. And his lack of keeping a job is another story. He does have a job coming up that I hope will help his depression by keeping him busy.

He will not clean, cook, or do house improvement or repairs unless I ask him. He might fix a door latch on his own but that is it. This really hurts me because our home is very old and a fixer-upper. When I try to do an improvement job for our home on my own, he gets upset. I have remodeled two homes before, so I know what I'm doing and have tons of ideas. I get no help from him and on top of it, I get yelled at if I make changes for the better. He gets upset when I am in the garage trying to organize my stuff and give some things away, yet he wants my mom's stuff out of there. So how can I sort through my mom's stuff and get it out if I can't go in there? I try to tell him this and it's like I am talking to a wall.

Also, he is very particular about items in the fridge. I did not buy the bottle of Heinz ketchup which fits into the door shelf. I bought the larger bottle, which does not fit. He showed me my mistake, huffed and puffed, let me know rather loudly that I bought the wrong size and walked away.

As he walked away, I said, "Do not talk to me as if I am a child. And my gosh, it isn't the end of the world. You know I am a bargain shopper and I will opt for a sale price over an it-fits-in-the-door price." Not sure if he heard a word I said.

He must be sure to tell me how to take care of the doors, handles, shelves, and racks in our oven and fridge. I've found that I must stand up to him, otherwise he gets very controlling over this. It's a kind of obsessive-compulsive disorder that is also common in autistic people.

Oh dear, I get tired of the adrenaline in my blood. I get tired of him staring at me doing a simple task because it's not 'his way'. He does the same thing to my son Devon and with his autism, well, I don't know how it affects my son. It's very concerning.

I get tired of anticipating what John will get upset over. It's like walking on eggshells. I don't respond well to controlling people. My mom was controlling and yelled most of the time. I guess I

84

found the familiar traits in John comforting in some way, but I know how unhealthy it is. I know I can't live like this. So, I'll work on the relationship because I cannot leave him, and I care deeply for him and love him. He has good sides to him that are endearing and loving, and people on the spectrum can't help it. I am aware of that thanks to what I have learned about my son.

John's upcoming full-time work gives me hope this will make him happier or otherwise occupied, and fingers crossed that he will pursue the counseling we plan to attend together.

One last challenge is that he almost always has an illness or an ache or pain that puts him in bed, so we'll see how long the job lasts.

I have hope that we can make this work, although some days I doubt. But honestly, I do love him. Despite all the difficulties, John is loyal, brilliant, funny, generous, and handsome. Those traits I adore, and I am doing all I can to keep him—and us—as happy as we can be.

* * *

River's comments:

I APPRECIATE APRIL'S willingness to lay everything out for us like she did. She gave us several very strong aspects of autism and how she handles the difficulties with John. The most profound is that she has a son with autism, yet *could not see it* in her husband. There is a lot of focus on children with autism, more so than adults.

I love her story because she expresses how much she wants to make the marriage work, and she's brave enough to fight through the good and bad times to understand her husband.

The part about trips being the most fun caught my attention because Gil and I have had a lot of fun on trips when they are *his* idea. When the world gets small and only Gil and I are together, things are easier. I think of it as being in his world. A trip can bring that feeling up because, for the most part, you are dependent on each other within a vacation. The time for events together may be set. I know Gil and I do best when the trip is planned in detail too. I sometimes hear how much fun neurodiverse couples have on trips. Our men are, I will just say it, big kids and when a schedule is going well and they can feel comfortable with you, a trip away with them can be a lot of fun.

Another point that April brought up was 'bossing'. This is at the top of the list of challenges for me in my relationship. A simple question that we feel to be a no-brainer can seem like a put-down to them. Or it's not in their schedule now to fill the dog bowl. If we tell them to do something, it feels threatening.

I continue to not understand this very well within my dynamics with Gil. He feels like anything I need from him is a demand and/or scolding. It's a tough one. Sometimes life gets 'real' and we need something right away. Or we may just want to vent to the person that lives with us day in and day out. A simple venting moment can be taken personally or be too emotional for Gil, and again I hear this often, for most men on the spectrum. This can come back to lack of reciprocity. Gil feels he is being scolded or commanded to do something because there is no talking about it. As in discussing something together and finding options or compromise.

April's example of the dog bowl is perfect. She was obviously hurting physically and simply wanted him to do something that needed to be done. He sounds like a bad person, but he truly doesn't understand she is hurting, and felt she was being demanding in having him do something that she noticed first and that she should be able to do herself. The simple act of filling a dog bowl became a huge unnecessary fight because April was hurting and needed help and he was not able to give it. No one is at fault; it's a difficult situation.

We could assume that John might feel frustrated that April is not well. But honestly, John is most likely thinking linearly: if she sees the dog bowl empty, then she should fill it. This comes back to mind blindness. He cannot put himself in her shoes and understand that she is hurting and unable to fill the bowl. Although it would be obvious to a NT person, since she is lying down with an ice pack, it is not obvious to John.

"Sorry that you made me say that to you." Oh, classic! Well, it is just perfect because yes, that is what he was feeling. Holding someone accountable is a tough one for many of us. And when that person truly doesn't understand his actions as being wrong, or not necessarily wrong but thoughtless, this can be a difficult situation for everyone.

After reading that part of April's story, I thought of a great short story from Dr. Brené Brown's *Shorts: Brené Brown on Blame* (YouTube). She said that one morning she was tired and dropped her coffee cup on the ground, and it smashed into bits. Immediately when it happened, she, in her mind, blamed her husband for breaking the mug. She had stayed up late waiting for him, so it was his fault she was tired, which resulted in her dropping the mug. She went on to teach us that many people like to blame for the sake of blaming but it usually comes from anger, which leads to not being able to express to someone else how they feel, down to feeling empathy for someone.

When I listen to her, I feel sad that I can only soak in her valuable lessons for myself, to help my relationship, but it would be very hard for Gil to grasp her teachings. She puts things simply and wonderfully, yet it is deep and involves a lot of thought into emotional bonds which I feel, for the most part—and I could be wrong—Gil will never fully grasp.

Now, on the flip side, if a person with autism is taught some of Brown's ways of relating to the world mechanically, it seems to help. Mechanically, meaning to show them scenarios with appropriate responses. Good actions by habit.

Many autistic adult men, who were not diagnosed young, are bullied or maybe even babied most of their lives. This creates other issues and personality disorders that could be avoided by understanding and teaching. There is much more to learn and luckily the schools are now recognizing autism earlier.

April mentions several times having to sound like a mom talking to a five-year-old child and often vice versa. I have many times had to put my foot down and remind Gil not to talk to me like I am five years old. Humans mimic their environment, and autistic mimicking is something they need to do, at times, to manage life—especially in a work environment. If Gil talks to me like I am five it's not that he is belittling me, although it certainly may seem that way, but it is more so from the conditioning he received as a child. He held onto that form of speech. It's almost oddly endearing that he is connecting with me as a family member. Most of the time I must talk to him very clearly since what would seem like common sense, Gil will not understand. I need to put it so clearly that I sound as if I am putting him down or belittling him. In other words, it goes both ways.

April told us how John is stuck in the 1950s style of child rearing. I gather, and this is only in retrospect, that if a person with autism cannot fully develop emotionally, that they can get emotionally 'stuck' at a young age. Gil was talked down to or ridiculed for being different, so that's what he does. John was taught in 1950s style so that's what he emulates. It's difficult enough for someone without autism to grow out of that mold, and many may not.

It's difficult for us to change. It's even more difficult for someone with autism to change.

I loved that April mentions a loving kind of talk and that sometimes they can sit down and calmly talk to one another. This is very good news.

Schedules! Working as a substitute teacher with special needs kids, I often walked into a classroom with autistic children and the staff truly understood schedules for them. They reinforced a consistent schedule. This is a good thing for the classroom, but life is not always on a schedule. For April, the schedule is brutal and along with it comes the dreaded OCD that occurs in a lot of autistic people. Issues like April's refrigerator challenge are common.

I saved the big one for last. Grief. Dear April, I am so sorry for your losses.

Grief is a tough one for all of us. How does an autistic person process grief when grief has so much to do with emotion? Let's remember how vast the spectrum is. Autistic people feel just as much sorrow and pain but may not show it in the same ways a NT person would. From my perspective within my experiences with Gil, expressing his emotions to others, and understanding what he is feeling, is most difficult. Asking Gil how he feels about anything doesn't usually yield an answer.

From what I've heard and experienced, expressing empathy to someone after they lose a person just doesn't happen with autistic people in a way that we can connect with. Not that they don't want to help. Usually they will give the shirt off their backs to help. The way that we use empathy is different. We may hold someone or cry with them. And many times, sure, stick our foot in our mouths too. Someone with autism may simply disappear in order to avoid the discomfort of the situation. Often, we might feel abandoned in a time that we need them most.

Gil didn't disappear, but when my dad passed—I'll never forget it—Gil said, "Why are you crying? I thought you didn't like your dad." Oh, how I wish I had known about his autism then. I felt that I had not been able to express the fact that I dearly loved my dad. It was just that at the end, my dad became angry and delusional. That is the time Gil met my dad. It stuck in his mind that my dad was bad, and I was angry. Nothing more.

Much like John still talks about his parents' deaths years later, so does Gil. After his parents died, he was almost cold about it. He had odd moments of tears, but he certainly cried a lot more when his dog died. The effect of losing a parent can go deep and possibly linger for years in someone that cannot express emotions well. A pet brings immense comfort to people because they don't have that capacity to judge us. Gil certainly missed his dog more than his parents. Not that he felt less pain when his parents passed, but his pet was a daily part of his life. If you've deeply loved a pet, you understand. I certainly do. The cats I had in my first marriage were like our kids, especially as each year went by that we couldn't conceive.

Gil loved his parents and could not express that deep emotional pain and loss in a way that 'normal' says we should. The processing time for grief is different for autistic people. I have a sad heart for people on the spectrum in this regard. Probably because I can't reach Gil and understand how he feels when I truly want to be there for him.

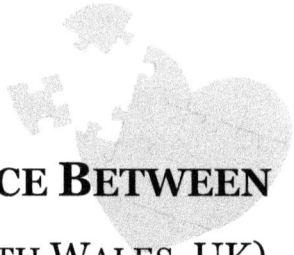

LIVING IN THE SPACE BETWEEN

MAGGIE'S STORY (NORTH WALES, UK)

YESTERDAY, AS I WALKED ACROSS TOWN TO my sister's house during the dead of night hoping she would let me in, I thought that when my grandmother was my age, she would have been retired and baking cakes for her grandchildren, not wondering how on earth she could go home and get through another day.

I awoke at six-thirty this morning. I'm not an early bird; in fact the endless task of having to process my day has meant staying up later and later until I lose the ability to sleep. Today, after only four hours of sleep, I find myself wide awake thinking about my story and needing to share it.

I realize as I write that I am writing for validation as much as to provide information. A need to communicate from a world where communication is difficult and gets shut down. A desperate need to be heard, but also a desire to help at least one woman get up and breathe every day, love herself, and realize that she is not losing her mind.

The year all this started had felt like a good year. Four years ago, my business was growing, I had had a wonderful sixtieth birthday celebration, and a new chapter was beginning.

I was developing a close community in my shop and I moved church so that I could get more involved in that area. It was there I met my husband Marco. When I was introduced to him, I found him intelligent, interesting and attentive. I used to look forward to bumping into him and wanted to know more about his personal life and Italian heritage.

After a couple of months of crossing paths with him, I found out that my previous husband had drowned. As a family we had been searching for him for years, and even though he and I had divorced, it was a devastating blow.

A couple of weeks following this terrible news, I got a text from Marco. He said he felt how awful it must be for me and had anyone come to see me? He asked how I was. I replied—honestly between sobs—that I was due to go to a friend's wedding that day and couldn't face it. I had been surviving on scones and jam and not getting out of bed for a week. Marco said he didn't know what to do to help but asked me if I wanted to go for a walk. I knew I needed to get some daylight and, because I was interested in him, I said yes. I didn't have much time to get ready, and it showed the state I was in that I threw some clothes on and let him pick me up.

I live near the sea and without even asking where I wanted to go, he took me to my favorite place. He was easy company walking along and seemed to be saying the right things, and he had got me out of the house. I was able to dump all that I felt, and because he was still a kind of stranger, it was easy to talk to him.

During the walk he stopped at a wall by the sea and told me that it was part of the sea defenses that he'd built, and I discovered he was a civil engineer.

Later, when we went on road trips, he would tell me about a road or a bridge or pier that he'd helped build.

After that first walk, he texted me every day to see if I was okay. It was good to have someone new to help me process my bereavement and make me feel cared for. There were more walks and little trips out.

I looked forward to his text messages. They contained songs to listen to, kind words, and snippets of Italian, his native tongue. They were comforting and attentive. (I wish I still had them. I lost them when I upgraded my phone. They were wonderful, and it wasn't like any other relationship I ever had. They would have reminded me of the man he was before we married, before he dropped his 'mask'.)

He remembers that time too, the same way that I do. He misses us from those days. Isn't that interesting? It's so easy for us, the NT partners, to forget that it was real and to think that somehow it was some deliberate plot to trap us. But I don't believe that. I think I was his special interest. Maybe he worked so hard because he was in love and scared of losing me? Now married, maybe simply sharing a space daily with me is too challenging? Whatever it is, sadly I now know that it is common to many women married to autistic men; the relationship changes greatly after marriage and it breaks our hearts.

After a while of dating, and becoming exclusive, the walks and road trips turned into meals out and him popping into my shop at lunch time to see me. Once he brought with him a massive tray of pastries, set them down on a table and walked straight out again, in front of my customers, without saying a word. My son thought it was so romantic that he did the same with his girlfriend and texted me to say that he was 'doing a Marco'. I wasn't the only one that was blown away by this relationship. My family and friends were too. His thoughtfulness and care for me were amazing. It seemed he couldn't do enough to help, always running around and doing things for me that he thought I would like.

As we grew closer, it was quite early in the relationship that Marco told me that he could see himself spending the rest of his life with me. I don't remember him asking me to marry him, nor me saying yes. It was as if he had the conversations in his head with me, and then made his own plans. As lovely as that felt to me in the beginning, him taking charge, these imagined conversations now cause huge problems in our marriage.

After two years of dating, we planned our wedding.

We waited until we got our own home before we lived together, and I moved in a week or two before we got married. I had thought that some of the little things I'd picked up from him were the usual pre-marriage stress, but I had no idea how drastically different it would be after we moved in together and were married, or that he had Asperger's. [The term Asperger's is still used in parts of the UK, although autism level 1 is becoming the preferred term globally.]

The change was dramatic and a real shock to me, as his constant attention to me was dropped and he seemed unable to comprehend what he was doing differently. He decided to sleep in a room on his own and had lots of routines and obsessions that I had not been aware of previously.

These daily routines and the strange way he lived were such a shock. How could I not know all this stuff about him?

Some of the things he did really upset me, but he didn't try to respond to my emotions as I sank deeper into this new mud. The only conclusion I could come up with was that he didn't care, and I couldn't make sense of that when I thought about how amazing and different our courtship had been. Now that I know so much about autism, I also know how common that story is. For nearly all of us, the dream disappeared overnight and made no sense.

I entered a world where we could no longer talk to each other. There was no such thing as a safe subject, as even a simple comment could drag us down a rabbit hole with no tools to get us out. He shut down and shut me out, stormed out a lot and shouted at me. I couldn't share how something made me feel. I would end up crying, in bits, on the floor and he could go to bed and sleep, leaving me there, and get up the next day as if nothing had happened.

At the time I didn't know what was going on, and our inability to discuss anything important in our marriage caused financial and health problems. I tried to get him to go somewhere with me for counseling, but the stress of that decision would lead to further meltdowns and arguments, so we never went anywhere. He hid away, then so did I. I was beginning to mirror his behavior as I tried to find some peace and, on the outside, we were fine—if no one got too close. I didn't understand how someone who seemed to love me, know me, and who had tried to make my dreams come true, could cut me off like this. Two years into our marriage I couldn't cope anymore and told all my troubles to a friend I bumped into while out shopping.

That year, we had decided to have the family over at our house for Christmas, but trying to sort it out became a nightmare and I couldn't take one more minute of the illogical, heartbreaking rows that had messed with my head, so I canceled Christmas.

I told him that he could go to his mother's and that I would move our Christmas party to my son's house. I felt like I couldn't take one more minute of him. I didn't care what I did, I just needed it all to stop. The constant rows and lack of empathy and support. The pressure of having to buy presents, because he didn't. The loneliness. The insane communication problems. Having to ask for everything because he controlled all the money yet got us into debt. It was all too much.

My husband dropped me off and opened his presents from my family there. I found that so hard, because that night I had wanted to tell my son how awful my marriage was and that I wanted to leave. Nevertheless, the hell of my relationship had been put on pause and over the next couple of days I could breathe a bit. I knew that I would have done anything to stay there and I really knew that my marriage was over.

After Christmas, I reluctantly went back to him and spent two days and nights researching the family tree, while simultaneously researching my husband's behavior and trying to work out why everything had changed, literally overnight, when I moved in and we got married.

During one of our rows, I realized that an absurd comment he made indicated that he had taken a common phrase literally, and I began to wonder. I had said that I was fed up with the mess in the house and was tempted to set fire to it all. He said that I couldn't do that because it wasn't safe and that he thought it was illegal. (Now that I know how literal he is, I must be so careful what words I use and that I make things, especially instructions, very clear.)

I started to really listen to how he talked to me. Tried out a few more phrases to check. I then realized, thanks to my special needs training as a teacher, that it might be autism. The veil fell off and for the whole of that day I could really see and hear him. I googled autism and marriage and came across an article on the Cassandra syndrome. I realized that the woman I was reading about was me.

I sat on this information for a couple of days. It was so hard to take in and I needed to think about what I could do. I found an online test for Asperger's and thought that if I was right, the result might give us an idea of what to do next. I carefully and calmly talked to him about our communication problems and got him to acknowledge how bad our marriage was. I told him that I felt that I would have to leave anyway so we had nothing to lose. It was scary for me because I was aware that if I was right, it would change us both and couldn't be undone.

To reassure him, I took the test too so that we could talk about the difference between the numbers. My score was 4, his was nearer 30. He surprised me by saying that his son had been diagnosed with alexithymia, which is a marked dysfunction in emotional awareness, social attachment, and interpersonal relations, which leads to a lack of empathy. A journey into seeing who we really were and seeking appropriate help had begun. We needed help living in the space between our very different worlds.

Marco's view of autism was very different from how he viewed himself. He struggled with the word. Asperger's seemed kinder to him, as the 'high functioning' element made him feel better. He keeps on telling me he is not thick. While he tried to come to terms with it, a great scream rose within me as I began to see how it really was between us, and I started grieving the loss of our perfect dream. I grieved the loss of the husband I expected to have, mixed up with how I had been swept off my feet by my knight in shining armor, and the contrast with our real life together. Immediately after we got married, life was so different to what I expected. Would I ever know the man I fell in love with again?

I talked to my family and friends. Read every book I could find. Joined online groups for wives with autistic husbands. In one of these groups, I met a lady who explained to me how his brain worked. She let me show him the article she had written. Marco found it interesting, and said he had thought that everyone's brains were like his. Now he could understand that his had developed in a different way to mine. He explained to me how he had to manually process each thought and consciously judge or choose it. How he had to think about the right answer. Was it what he thought? What answer was I looking for from him? He couldn't understand how I could just talk without thinking.

Moments of clarity regarding the space between us do not come very often. I wish he could hold on to those revelations and build on them. His very poor short-term memory, tendency to take offense at every word, and his own defense mechanisms often undo any progress we make. He moves between acceptance and denial constantly. It is so difficult for us to have comfortable discussions.

While he tried to process and deal with his own preconceived ideas about autism, I became an observer. My experience as a special needs teacher easily joined the dots, but I wasn't really prepared for how it shocked my system, as I started to see my husband in a new way that I realized I couldn't undo. It is what it is. The veil had fallen away from my eyes and while it gave me some answers, and in some way a sense of relief, it was not a comfortable experience and left me feeling that I had lost the man I had fallen in love with.

That first observation about him taking me literally made me really focus on what he had understood me to be saying, and as I listened and watched I noticed other communication problems. I noticed that he would flip what I said so that if I asked if *he* wanted a cup of tea, he would say, "Of course I'll make you one."

Often when he talked to me, he would start a sentence with 'they' or 'it'; clearly, he had a thought in his head he hadn't shared, and I had no way of knowing what he was talking about and had to ask him endless questions to find out. Also, he seemed to have conversations in his head with me and make a lot of presumptions about my motives and what I had said based on these imaginary conversations.

The lack of empathy, or even any kind of response, is the hardest thing to accept. It means that I am living a lonely life with no connection, and he will never understand how decisions can be based on an emotion. I can tell him the most dreadful things about my life and he never comments or ask me questions about it. My husband often doesn't show any reaction, never mind empathy, shock, or concern.

Knowing that he can't read me is one thing; trying to read him has its own difficulties. I can't rely on what he says. Often, he will lie if he fears he is in trouble. He will say things that really hurt or are not actually what he thinks. The volume of his voice doesn't give me a clue, because his voice can get louder and louder and he is unaware that he is shouting.

Sometimes I think that I need to read the physical signs more. If he is really stressed during an argument, apart from shouting and walking out, and taking offense at absolutely everything, I noticed his eye would twitch or he would rub his head. His facial expressions don't always seem to match what he is saying. He would smile at inappropriate moments, which either freaks me out or makes me mad.

I had fondly thought of him as a mad professor when we were courting. His formal language made him seem a lot older than me even though I was eight years his senior. Once, when we were leaving my son's house, Marco shook his hand and said, "Nice to see you." My son looked at me oddly because we were leaving, and my husband had known him for four years and my son called him Dad. I quickly realized, looking at him through my new eyes, that he had learned a lot of these social graces because it was difficult for him to know how to react intuitively in a situation. Because of the alexithymia part of Asperger's, he can't put himself in someone else's shoes. Often, I have had to distract him away from a conversation because he is happily talking about work, his voice getting louder, and not noticing that the person he is talking to has switched off and is feeling uncomfortable.

Apart from the lack of empathy and normal conversations, I am constantly thrown off balance by unexpected things he might ask or say to me that fly at me from out of nowhere.

Right now, after sitting down to continue writing, my heart is racing thinking of an escape plan. This happens so often and it's the thing that I struggle with most. This morning I woke, switched the kettle on in my bedroom and it wouldn't come on. Checked a bedside lamp and nothing. He is working from home now as we are in a Covid lockdown. He has the habit of only putting a partial payment on the electric meter, so I told him he needs to check it. He grunted at me and then flipped fuses downstairs. The light came on. Went off again and I told him it is off again.

He said, "It must be something you have done."

I'd been asleep doing nothing. (We enter the meltdown dance. Back and forth.) I calm my talk. He shouts and screams in an abusive tone. Blames me. "YOU YOU." He tells me I never do what I'm told. I tell him I'm not a child and he is not my parent. I tell him again I have done nothing. I've been asleep. I ask him again to unplug anything he has been using. SLOWLY switch the fuse switches. Eventually they work. He hates being wrong. He never voluntarily apologizes in the moment. I say that I don't think I want to talk to him today and walk away.

When he is at home all day, I wake with dread. I never know what will kick off out of the blue. I guess this morning his anger was because he couldn't fix it. Maybe he didn't want to feel stupid. Who knows? I only know that I've been screamed at when I was innocent. That my neighbors are probably wondering why I stay and if this is all my fault.

I retreat. Handling these tough times is difficult. There is constantly the need to detach, observe, lie to self. If I can do this, he may have a better day, but I may not. Other days the hurts and frustrations are too much, and I say too much, dump too much, and feel desperately alone. Friends rarely understand what my marriage is really like, yet I need them. I need a look from someone that validates my feelings, care wrapped around my heart. A space to be and breathe.

Lockdown brings the reality to surface. We were allowed a 'bubble' at one point and I was able to visit my sister. It had been such a long time since I could just be me, without thinking, editing, treading on eggshells. I couldn't remember the last time I had laughed, and when I came home, I sobbed silently in my room, because for a couple of hours with my sister, I had found myself again.

He doesn't cope in tough times at all. He will panic, get depressed, get angry if he is anxious. He will avoid tasks, not open letters or plan anything that he needs to do. His fear of failure feeds his procrastination. (Today he texted me to say that he must be brave and come back into the room instead of walking out and avoiding issues.)

It's so difficult to discuss anything with him and help him think things through. I try and ask him if what he is thinking is true? Is it presumption or fear? What does he need to find out? These conversations rarely go well because it is hard to calm him down, and his behavior can range from scary aggressive to childish tantrums, with a lot of walking out or going to bed to sleep. If I work hard enough at discarding my own needs, he can have a good day. But it is rarely a good day for me unless I put in the work. I need a lot of self-care and reaching out to others. I must tell myself to behave as if I lived alone; what would I do for me then?

Life with Marco is so unpredictable. At times he seems calm, kind and likeable. Runs around doing little things to help, which are often part of the many routines he has. He told me that when I let him, or ask him, to help me it makes him happy. I often hear him humming to himself when he is making me a cup of tea.

One thing that helps us is my understanding of some of his habits and routines. I think that doing the same things every day gives him a sense of achievement and security. Also, it is helpful if I want to get his attention or develop a new habit in our marriage, that I attach it somehow to his routine and work with it.

For instance, he comes home early on Friday, so I picked Friday as a date night. So, he knows it is date night because it's the day everyone goes home early. He always brings me water and a drink to my room every night. When I found that I needed more space at the end of the day, I made the drink myself so that I could be on my own, and because he was disappointed I had changed the routine, he got the message and started respecting my boundaries.

His thinking can be very black and white and depends on the rules he has learned or made up for himself. He often talks about the right thing to do. This can be honorable and make him loyal and dependable. But it can also make him inflexible, controlling, and produce a lot of anger if we are trying to discuss new thoughts or ideas or trying to break down what has happened in an argument. If an argument is getting out of hand, I find sometimes I can take advantage of his attention to detail and distract him by mentioning something in the room or a noise I can hear. His poor short-term memory will often mean that he doesn't return to the subject, so we can move on.

In difficult conversations I must try to hold both of his hands, look him in the eye and soften my voice, to help him stay in the conversation and not run away. Sometimes that works. Other times it adds fuel to the fire.

It can take him a very long time to process something I've said or something that has happened. In real time, he needs a pretty long space to think before he answers a question. He can't just answer. He needs to analyze it and think of all the possibilities and get comfortable that the answer is the right answer and won't get him into trouble. He has such anxiety about any confrontation or questioning, so much so that it will trigger imaginary conversations as he tries to guess what you are going to say, and he always finishes your sentences. This makes it so hard for him to have normal conversations that are in any kind of flow, especially if he can't read the social clues that would tell a neurotypical person that it's someone else's turn to speak or that we should ask some questions.

This long processing time is something you really must make room for with an autistic person. The effort involved is huge. If I can be patient enough, he may get back to me a week later about something we have talked about, and surprise me by what he has thought about, understood, and shared. I think that a lot of conversations we had when we were courting were special because he had time to think about them and text me. He can write and share amazing things if I can persuade him to write to me. He also says that writing helps him think and process and sort out stuff. I wish that he would make that a daily practice. I have also noticed that we can discuss things better over the phone and I will even ring him in the house, if we are in separate rooms, to take the risk out of difficult subjects. Often, he will share on a more emotional level then too. I think that eye contact and being confused by our facial expressions may not help autistic partners.

The biggest problem in our marriage is the lack of emotional support and response. It is hard that he cannot read my face, and that his face shows such little expression. I must ask for what I need as a response, which takes away the sense that it was given to me. It means that he may feel love or kindness, but *I won't know it*. I used to be amazed that he could cry over a sad cartoon, but not recognize that I was devastated by an event in my life.

The lack of connection makes intimacy difficult. It is hard to feel close to someone who doesn't talk or look at you when they touch you, especially when they don't even notice your lack of response. Interestingly, it was quite different before we got married. We felt close and connected then. This huge change in behavior can make me resentful at times. I even rejected a hug this morning because it came out of the blue when we were arguing. It felt inappropriate that he wanted to touch me right then. I apologized when I realized that it was his way of responding because he couldn't find the words. To him, a hug is his response, while I needed words and validation.

I must really look for the gold in the dress each day. The kind and loving, thoughtful things he will do that made me fall in love with him. His love language is acts of service. Mine, sadly, is words of affirmation.

There are times that I really like him. Little things that maybe remind me of how I used to think he was amazing. He notices such detail: the necklace I'm wearing, a different nail polish. Once he blew me away by saying, "Your perfume fills the car with you. It's wonderful."

He is so interesting to talk to and his long-term memory is so detailed, while his short-term memory has advantages on days we really stuff up. He has an almost childlike ability to reset and forgive each day.

I must make a real effort to be really encouraging and supportive and try to show him he is still a man with choice, and that it's not all about autism. I must make it obvious that I am committed to him and working with him, and I must show that in a practical way because he remembers that more than words. He once told me that he could tell that I loved him when we were courting, because I bought a little table for my flat so that we could sit and have dinner together, and look into each other's eyes across the candlelight. He said that it meant so much to him. We have been together four years and he told me this out of the blue last week. Moments like that, where I get a glimpse into his heart, mean so much.

We may never arrive at the perfect marriage, but I hope that I can stay on board and enjoy the journey.

* * *

River's comments:

THE BEGINNING OF **Maggie's story** reminded me of the fact that my mom was never in this kind of situation either. There is no training available or knowledge of how to make a relationship like ours work. It's like a deep secret hidden from the world.

When I asked women in the Facebook groups to write their stories, most were very concerned about privacy. Many simply couldn't bring up the past because it was too painful. Many were afraid of their husband's career being affected if anyone found out. That feeling that we must keep the autism secret is disturbing to me. Very disturbing. The lack of awareness goes on and on, while more and more couples suffer needlessly.

All the women I meet within these groups are kindred spirits. We can come together and talk and be heard. However, we need the 'normal' world as well. You can only sit and talk about how life is insane and crazy for so long. The awareness must get out there. We can't keep sitting by and living in this cave of fear, resentment, and denial. Our husbands can change but, for the most part they will not change as much as we must change. We'll always do most of the heavy lifting. But even with that daunting fact, the secrecy is the worst part. We can't keep hiding because the cycle will continue. We need support from the outside world, the ability to be open with family and friends so we all can work together. That is my message.

As Maggie did, I have asked the same question over and over. Why am I in this situation? What did I do that was so horrible as to have this insanity in my life? However, imagining conversations is something I hadn't thought of before. As I read her story, I thought about how Gil has said things that he was sure he had told me before. Like sometimes, he will come to me and say "I told you about that situation and you agreed with me" when I have not a clue what he is talking about.

Again, the holidays and events are often difficult. I remember having a Christmas party one year, after a lot of work to get Gil to agree to even having it, and right before the party, he took off all my decorations on a table. It was a gift table I'd spent a long time preparing. I asked why and he said, "We don't need that." I proceeded to put it all back right before people arrived. It was very nerve-wracking. I know that if I didn't understand autism at that time, I would have lost it. But you do what you must do.

Maggie mentions the flipping in conversations. I have experienced this as well, but it is so subtle with Gil that I can't think of a good example. I feel Maggie shares perfectly how it happens.

There has been many a time that I want something different than he does. But because he wants it, then I must want it. Take food, for example. I love peanut butter. He hates it. I can't mention peanut butter without him giving me a gag response every time. I get it but it is constant and gets old.

We often, and I hear this in Maggie's story and in all the others, feel that we're never totally at rest. There is always something around the corner to deal with. It's exhausting. Even when times are good, I know a crash is coming. After over a decade with Gil, I still have moments when I want to leave him. Now, I think many couples, neurodiverse or not, go through this but I feel that for us, there is a different level of anguish that we feel and it never seems to fade.

Gil can never apologize either, as Maggie mentioned in her story. Is it a guy thing? Maybe, although I don't think so. Often, an autistic man truly feels that everything he does is right. If Gil accidently steps on my foot, he will apologize. If Gil says something that hurts my feelings, it is my challenge that it hurt, and he is not at fault so what is the purpose of apologizing when he has done nothing wrong? It's logical to him.

Like I've said before, we need the outside world. Maggie mentions that seeing her sister helped her to feel normal her again. We need the world to see us and understand us. Luckily Maggie's sister gives her joy. Many families and friends blame us for the issues in our relationships because they can't understand what it is truly like. You have to *live* it!! We get it; we simply want the support that comes from people knowing we're in a more challenging relationship, one that isn't the norm. We are in a neurodiverse relationship and if we choose to stay, we don't want pity and neither does our partner.

D. River Martin

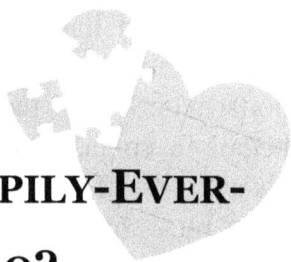

WHERE DID HAPPILY-EVER-AFTER GO?

WENDY'S STORY

PETER AND I MET IN A EUROPEAN COUNTRY more than thirty years ago. We are both Americans and happened to have a common acquaintance also living in that country. When we met, I wasn't sure if he was sixteen or twenty-two; he seemed childlike in a way and looked like he had only recently begun to shave. Upon further discussion, I found he had just graduated college. He was different from anyone I had ever met. At once like a big kid doing goofy things and then a man of superior intelligence, with a photographic memory, highly sensitive, musical, and deeply spiritual. He was very into God and I was there conducting Bible studies for U.S. military personnel.

I came from a broken home and went through rebellious teen years. I had fallen in love with Jesus and meeting a nice guy who liked to talk about spiritual things was new to me. We had a core group of friends that all hung out together. The whole group of us had Bible studies, went on trips exploring

115

Europe, and had a great time. Through unrelated circumstances, Peter moved into a spare room of the house where I was living with an American family. We began to spend more time together and he would always talk of his relationship with God not being what he wanted it to be . . . and he cried a lot. He would take handfuls of coins to the phone booth and call his folks and sob on the phone as he told them of his struggles with God, and they reassured him of his conversion at age ten and that he was okay.

He paid special attention to me and was very desirous of the same relationship that I had with God. He said friends had asked him why he didn't just marry me. He told me he didn't know why not, and we got engaged. In hindsight, I see his depression, and strange instances where he would seemingly ignore important things I was saying and turn the conversation back to himself. In my immaturity, I just thought he was a 'sold-out seeker of Jesus'. These were red flags that I ignored—thinking all would be well when we married and lived happily ever after. I could not have been more wrong. After we married, he became lost in his own head. Saying "I love you" to me became "Do I really love Wendy?" and "What is love?" until I was non-existent . . . just a part of his never-ending thought bubble.

His depression became more and more pronounced and seemed to focus on his relationship with God, or lack thereof. Looking back, this was likely his special interest and had been since age ten. Through it all I remained his biggest fan and best cheerleader. Always a listening ear, cheering him on, and doing whatever I could to keep whatever straw might break the proverbial camel's back from landing on him.

Five kids and twenty-two years later found him unwilling or unable to work anywhere but a minimum wage job despite an adoring, helpful wife and many mouths to feed.

One day I heard that a café in a nearby tourist town was for sale and let him know. We had lived above a café in Europe when we were first married. Then we owned a small café for ten years in the States. Peter is a phenomenal chef and we ran that restaurant until we had our fourth child. He didn't manage his time well and the pressure of the work seemed to be killing him. Now, years later, upon hearing of the new opportunity he lit up vibrantly. More vibrancy than I had seen in him in a long, long time. We brought on partners and bought the café, though I saw red flags that I once again ignored.

Even though I was home educating our children, I worked long hours to renovate this restaurant and help him have a career he could feel good about. Within a year, the partnership had gone sour and an emergency meeting was called. On the way to the meeting I asked my husband to please have my back. I sensed I was going to be used as the scapegoat . . . and I was. And my husband didn't say a word. I tried talking with him about it afterward and he would say nothing—he just had a 'deer in the headlights' sort of look. I set up a marriage counseling session right away, as this felt big. Twenty-two years of being his cheerleader and he couldn't seem to have my back this one time when I specifically asked him to.

The business partners moved on but the cooks he hired were even less desirable. One day after closing, a cook began to yell "fuck you" at me. I managed 'front of house' and my husband managed the 'back of house'. (Restaurant lingo for the waitstaff and cooks/dishwashers respectively). Since it was his jurisdiction, I went to my husband to let him know what was going on. He called the cook staff and me over and proceeded to let them yell profanities at me while he just stood there. He loved to be loved by the staff and he seemed to be entranced by it all. I still had cleaning to do with the waitstaff, and kids to get home to, so I excused myself and went back to work. This became a pattern. I would have fired them myself, but I knew my husband would rehire them the next day and things would be even worse. After a few years of this I asked for an amicable divorce. He was shocked. He did not have any idea that there was anything wrong.

But an amicable divorce was out of the question for him. He would not talk about any of it with me, but what he would do was say lots to the children. We had gone to the child advocacy class together, but it seemed whatever they would tell us NOT to do, he would do. I had my lawyer work out a sweet deal in which he would keep the business and we would share the house so the kids would have their familiar home, and we would round-robin a week at a time being there with them. He would have none of it. He hired a crafty lawyer that was milking him for all we were worth. He was hiding money, was going to fight for full custody, and I could see bankruptcy on the horizon.

One evening as I was holding two sick children, one in each of my arms, and trying to sleep in a twin-size bed, I realized that I couldn't go through with it. I could not put the kids through this . . . so I called off the divorce.

Raw and reeling, one bright light was sparked. We hired a consultant for the café. Even though my husband is an awesome chef, it was becoming very evident that he is an awful businessman. One of the first things this professional did when he came in was to fire all insubordinate staff! He also talked my husband into giving me a paycheck each week as well as get life insurance so the kids and I wouldn't be financially burdened if anything happened to him. (Two things that I asked my husband for until I was blue in the face, to no avail). This is often very common with autistic partners.

I begged for marriage counseling and he finally consented to go. Three marriage counselors later and not much has changed. Each time, he refused to do the homework the counselor would give us, felt no need to take the things the counselor said seriously, and was always done with it all if the counselor did not agree with him. To this day, I don't know if it was the counseling or the money it cost that he hated the most. The last marriage counselor lasted the longest and that is the one that I paid for all myself. We stopped going because of a move but at the last session, both the counselor and I were very disheartened. It was so blatant that if Peter was talking, he was highly engaged. But if the counselor or I had the floor he went into his own little world, or fell asleep.

I had never been an ultimatum giver, but it seems to be the only thing that works with him. So last winter I told him that he needed to get a psychological evaluation. He consented when he found out that insurance would indeed pay for it.

The other ultimatum that I gave was that I finally would be taking over our personal finances. He would refuse to talk about it with the marriage counselor. For our entire marriage he oversaw the finances. He is awful at it. He thinks it is no big deal to pay a bill late. He thinks I am a frivolous spender, even though I show him the receipts: shampoo, maxi-pads, gas, kids' clothes. This is often attributed to the mind-blindness that seems to go with autism.

There are so many strange stories I could tell. For many years I thought that I must be the one with a problem. One of the best things I ever did was to get counseling for myself. To begin to get to know myself and my worth. To realize that it was okay for me to stand up for myself and our children. I had been so careful, trying to keep those straws off his back, that the kids and I were last in everything. And it almost cost me my life.

Two years ago, I almost died. It was the perfect

storm of lack of self-care, stress, a virus, and an uncontrolled autoimmune disease. I woke sick to my stomach on a day our restaurant was closed, and I just thought it was a virus going around. I could not get my blood sugar under control even though I had eaten nothing that day. I was becoming delirious and voice-messaged some girlfriends who could hear the danger in my voice and told me to go to the emergency room right away. Even though Peter was home, he was not answering my phone calls or texts. (Which is quite 'normal' for him.) My oldest son did answer, however.

I saw my husband on the stairs and told him what was going on and asked for his help to get to the car. I can still hear my then fourteen-year-old daughter continuously ask her dad, incredulously, if he was going to take me. He said no. That it was too much work to get my son out of the driver's seat.

The ER staff had me taken by ambulance to the big city hospital thirty-five minutes away. There, I found myself in one of those out-of-body experiences where I was seemingly looking down on my near-comatose body with the hospital staff in the Cardiac ICU. They kept asking me questions and I could not get my brain and my mouth to line up. I was giving them odd answers, things like my doctor's name from twenty years ago. I kept praying to God that they would not send me to the psych unit. I was alone, as Peter chose to go watch a movie with the restaurant staff even though we had an agreement to not fraternize with them. We had fought about it the night before.

During that week in the hospital (five days in ICU, two in a regular room), my husband came once to see me. It was late, after his 'movie night' the first night, and he never came back again. Not even to bring me home after I was released. (The kids would tell me later that they asked to come see me or to at least pick me up and he wouldn't bring them.) I vowed that if I did live through this, things would have to be different.

It was around that same time that an acquaintance asked me if I had ever thought my husband might have Asperger's. I then remembered that I had read a short article about it and how they had trouble recognizing faces. It reminded me of my husband very much. I began reading everything I could about autism. The more I read, the more the dots were connecting. Like a movie being played out before my eyes, all the pieces of the strange puzzle of our lives began to fall into place and make sense.

You see, if a person is unaware they are in a neurodiverse relationship like this, it can often lead to mental harm which can lead to physical illness or distress. I would say that knowledge has been empowering. Though it has taken two years to get Peter on board, I myself have done a lot of research and counseling. I am better able to understand and not take his atypical ways personally. Now I am my children's and my best advocate. We are worth taking care of and I make sure that whatever we need, happens. My husband does not stand in the way of what needs to be done . . . he just can't seem to think of these things himself.

For instance, at the restaurant when I was being vilified, Peter thought I was strong enough to handle any personal attacks against me. I think I likely was. The thing I wasn't strong enough for, was that my husband would not have my back. The person I gave my heart, soul, and body to could stand there and seemingly relish it happening. The one I had cheerleaded for, daily encouraged, inexhaustibly stood by. If I had been anywhere else alone, I could have handled that kind of verbal abuse and let it roll like water off a duck's back.

It was not what other people were saying to or about me. The profanities yelled at me; the fingers pointed. Sure, it stung . . . but the searing pain was that my husband had no problem with it. At certain points, even seemed to invite it. He had told me once that he didn't like conflict, but that he enjoyed watching it. I felt like someone thrown into the coliseum and my husband a goading voyeur, reveling in the agony of the moment. Me, not being seen by him as a person.

I turn my heart, soul, body, spirit, life to you, dear God. But why would I ever turn it back over to him?

* * *

River's comments:

How resilient Wendy is to have kept going, to keep

123

her family safe at all costs. Even almost at the cost of her life. What I take from this story is the absolute importance of finding answers. Why does he do the things that he does? Why the absentness, aloofness, seeming not to care, the 'bad behavior' and immaturity. The lack of acknowledgement or, as Wendy put it, how he didn't have her back.

The 'mind blindness' in all our men is a common thread that we fall back on in order to understand them better. And this makes sense because a relationship is mostly about the ability to see another person's point of view. To walk in another person's shoes and to acknowledge a partner's position. I feel that for the most part (again, it's a spectrum), someone who is high functioning / low needs learns tricks to get around that lack of being able to put themselves in our shoes. That is where the gaslighting comes in, and where not having our backs plays in. It can leave us doubting ourselves and feeling insecure, which can lead to the uncertainty of all that we hold dear, which may lead to ill health and often does. It's why the wives/partners often say that they feel crazy.

I must touch on the fact that it is worrisome for children in that environment, particularly girls, like Wendy's daughter. They may grow up and feel it is okay for men to behave badly, such as the time Peter didn't take her mom to the hospital. This is a scary truth when raising children in this environment. It is extremely important for the kids, as well, to understand why their dad may act this way. Things may have been much different if they had known.

Possibly Wendy would not have gotten so ill. Knowing what is going on with your spouse/partner can not only help your children immensely but may even save your life.

When the average person thinks of special interests, we think of maybe a hobby or the pursuit of a specific goal. But people on the spectrum focus in on one thing and it becomes their life ... sometimes more so than their partner or family.

I have to applaud Wendy for keeping her family safe instead of going into a black hole, like she very well could have and with good reason. Now, with her better understanding of her husband, she can breathe a little easier.

D. River Martin

HOW DO YOU KNOW
WHEN HE'S THE ONE?

LAUREN'S STORY

I MET MY HUSBAND NOAH ON A dating website. I was a kindergarten teacher working in an elementary school, and it wasn't the ideal place to meet a man. I decided to message him on the website, and he didn't reply for almost three weeks. When he finally replied, he called me and made plans to meet the same evening. Our first date was dinner and a movie, and I remember finding him very attractive but there was something 'off' that I couldn't put my finger on.

We went to dinner at a hibachi restaurant. They weren't known for having the best desserts, so I passed. Instead of getting the check, he ordered himself a scoop of vanilla ice cream. I thought it was a bit odd, but it was clear he didn't care. He happily sat there and ate his ice cream while I waited. I didn't think much more about it and by the end of the night we had a kiss and said goodbye. I liked him and was instantly attracted to him.

From that night on, we moved quickly. On our

127

second date I remember him talking a lot. It felt like he was rambling, but I thought he was probably just nervous. He made a comment about talking a lot and I thought, *He definitely doesn't know me.* I'm infamous for talking too much but he never really got to see that side of me early on because for the most part, he took center stage. It came off as confidence, and I found that attractive.

For the record, he is truly NOT a talker. Or I should say, not a communicator. I even sensed this when he made that comment on our second date, but I brushed it off. Our conversations never flowed like they did when I would talk to a friend. You get a vibe that they are on the same page as you, know what you're about to say, and agree excitedly. With Noah, we talked, but it was more informational stuff that he would tell me. I would talk and he'd comment back but it just didn't flow.

Back then, I had no idea what a man with autism looked like. He was all the things I was looking for in a man, and I had no reason to believe that his social skills were underdeveloped. On the days that followed our first date, we spoke every day, all day. A week later we went to Universal Studios in Orlando. He seemed a bit childish on the trip, but I thought I was just being too critical of him. We were, after all, at a theme park and he was excited. He was a nice, respectful, handsome man. There was no reason for me to sabotage what we had simply because he was acting childish. That was how he showed his excitement. It came off as odd, but again it was no reason to break up with him.

That weekend he said, "I love you." I wasn't ready to say it back, but man did it make me feel special. Three weeks after we met, my lease ended, and I moved into his townhouse. He had a great job, was super smart, and seemed to want all the same things that I did in the future. It seemed like the right move.

Once we started living together, I really got to know him. I saw that he was used to sleeping with his laptop in bed. I was told that people at work thought he was sick or depressed and they were worried about him because he wasn't working around the clock anymore. His work had been his passion and I felt special that he turned that passion towards me instead.

Looking back, I know now that he was hyperfocused on work, which happens to be his special interest. I suppose I also became his special interest. I didn't say 'I love you' back to him until about three months after our first date. I was honest with him that maybe I couldn't ever say it. I didn't know yet how I was feeling. He was brokenhearted when he heard this, but eventually I said to him, "I love you." Saying those three words meant, to me, that Noah and I would spend the rest of our lives together.

I remember taking a walk with my mom and asking her, "How do you know when they are 'the one'?" I wasn't sure. He was a great guy who checked all the boxes. Intelligent. Handsome. Wants kids.

Why would I just walk away from that? So, I didn't.

Six months after we met, he proposed. We were supposed to meet up for the first time with my good friend and her husband at the beach. But Noah woke up with a task on his mind. When I reminded him of our plans he wasn't on board. I was shocked that he'd think it was socially acceptable to cancel last minute for no reason. He told me he had something special to get. And made it obvious it was an engagement ring. He drove us to his work, and when he got the ring he returned to the car and showed me a peek of a turquoise Tiffany bag from his pocket. I thought it was odd that he would do that. Fifteen-minute ride home, we are sitting in the car in the driveway and he looks at me with a panicked-looking face, takes the ring out of his pocket and says, "Will you marry me?"

It was odd and not how I envisioned it, but I said yes. Nothing felt right about it. I later found out the ring was fake when I went to the mall with a friend and had the Tiffany store look at it. He had been so defensive when I made comments about the ring early on, and I was anxious and confused. This confirmed my suspicions and almost ended our relationship. To this day he swears he bought it on eBay and had no idea it was fake. He couldn't find the paperwork anywhere. Who buys a ring on eBay, anyway? He chalked it up to cultural differences. In his country, women didn't get a diamond. And proposing wasn't a huge magical production like it is here in the United States.

We got married in 2010. He wasn't very

attentive anymore. I thought maybe he had ADHD. At one point I suspected he was a narcissist since everything he said was twisted, confusing, and I was always made to believe it was my fault. He also had other difficult personal challenges that affected us negatively. He had sensory issues, including his wedding ring, as well as many other things including clothes and food. He wears the same shirts and shorts that are super soft. He won't wear a button down or polo shirt.

Food-wise, he's the pickiest eater I have ever met. I'd say he doesn't eat 80% of foods. I, on the other hand, am a foodie. So, this is a huge compromise for me! Not being able to share sushi, pad thai, or spinach dip appetizer crushes my soul. Therefore, I love having nights out with my girlfriends. We order the most delicious food and share everything. It makes me happy and fulfilled. Sometimes I must get what makes me happy from others. And I've learned to be okay with that.

Our first son was born in 2012 and he was the most difficult child you could ever imagine. Cried like he was dying, and it never stopped. He was never happy. He never slept. I spent my days researching my baby and my husband. I was living in a world I didn't understand. It wasn't until my son was five that he was diagnosed with Autism Spectrum Level 1 (mild). It was around the same time that I realized this was the answer to everything I struggled with about my husband. I finally understood. My husband was on the spectrum, too. I saw that around others, he could get on well, but at home he struggled to be a husband and dad. We fought a lot. I felt crazy. Out of control. Alone. This carried on for years. I had a friend come over to see my son as a baby and my husband came home from work and went straight to his computer, and didn't even say hello to our son.

My bold friend looked at him and said, "Get off your laptop and say hello to your son!" He was appalled. I agreed with her and he was fuming.

When she left, he said, "How dare she speak to me like that in my own home." I agreed but I was so glad others saw what I saw and spoke out. I was usually too afraid because I didn't want to fight.

Fast forward ten years, six houses, seven cars, and three kids later (did I mention my husband has impulse control issues?) and we end up in a dark place. Filled with years of resentment and misunderstandings. My husband has absolutely no family nearby and he doesn't have any friends or connections with anyone outside of me and our kids. It's not that he doesn't want friends, but he has trouble maintaining a relationship with someone. Things like calling them back, answering texts, making plans and following through with them are challenging for him.

In February we went on a family cruise and the day we returned he dropped me and the kids off at home. During that drive home, he talked about how busy his day was going to be and all the team members he needed to pick up from the airport. He said he'd be working late all week, and this was nothing new to me.

That night I tucked the kids into bed and went to sleep without him. He's spent many nights out until 2-3 AM over the years without much communication at all so when I hadn't heard from him, I wasn't worried. But when I woke up at 6 AM and realized he never came home, I tried calling him and texted everyone, but his phone was off. I took my kids to school and at 8:30 AM I finally got a text from him. It said that he did something that ruined our family and how sorry he was. He told me he got drunk and his friend took him to a hotel to sleep it off.

My husband? Drunk? The guy who doesn't drink. What in the world? My husband didn't come home all day. He didn't even come home to shower or say how sorry he was. I was distraught.

When he finally came home later that evening, he sat down and said, "I cheated on you."

My whole world crumbled upon hearing those words. My husband. The man incapable of even having eyes for another woman, cheated on me. A past work colleague he had kept in touch with over the years was in town for business the day we got back from our cruise. He never mentioned the amazing vacation he'd just had with his family, but instead offered to pick her up from the airport when she arrived. He never told me he had plans in his calendar to have dinner with only her. He decided to drink and managed to sit there for almost seven hours. They went back to her hotel and well . . . . He woke up, took a shower and went to work. Everyone thinks their husband would never. I was that woman until that day. He was broken and unhappy and made a monumental mistake. I forgave him.

Nine months later we almost separated. He detached himself from me for months. Then a simple text from me changed everything all over again. 'Have you talked to Betsy?' The woman he'd slept with. He simply replied 'Yes, recently I have.' And my whole world crumbled all over again.

He thought it was okay because we were getting separated and didn't see the issues I had with it. I had to explain to him that we are living under the same roof and we solve our issues privately together. I had told him that he was never to talk to Betsy again under any circumstances and yet, she's the first person he reached out to when he felt hurt and lost. A desperate attempt to feel loved. I believe he remembers how I struggled to say I love you when our relationship began. He claims to this day that I don't truly love him like he loves me. Even with all the pain, we got through it and are still together.

We have three crazy amazing kids and Noah is a good dad. He's always willing to engage with them. Even so, there are annoying mishaps that occur. One Friday he offered to pick up our son, who was at grandma's house, and bring him home. I texted him to make sure he would be there on time since he worked an hour away. I asked, 'Can you get Reed at four?'

Noah texted 'yes'.

At 3:40 I sent him a reminder text. 'Did you

leave?'

His reply? 'No, I'm leaving at 4'.

I responded, 'I said get him at 4, not 5' (1 hour commute).

Noah, 'I thought I was to leave at 4'.

I said 'Who tells you the time to leave? I don't know your exact commute to her house. When someone asks you to get them, they tell you the time they need you to get them. Not the time they need you to leave. That doesn't make sense'. (This has happened many times.) Crickets . . . . Him 'Well I'm leaving now' (3:45).

My response 'Text me when you are on your way'. Because let's be real, I know he's not leaving yet.

He texted 'OK. I'm calling for my car now'. At 3:51 he calls the valet as this is how he parks for the building he works in.

I wait and check in again. 'What's going on? It's 4:20'.

He's flustered now and responded 'It's not my fault it's taking the car almost 40 minutes to come! It always takes this much time around this time of day! Crucify me!'

I replied, 'If you knew it took that long why didn't you ask for it at 3:30 if you planned to leave at 4?'

The situation only went downhill from there and he was upset with me, because naturally it's my fault he picked our son up at 6 o'clock instead of 4 from grandma's house! These kinds of things always happen and looking back you always think, *How did*

I not avoid this? I should have known. This is a scenario of blame shifting when he was running late but somehow, he cannot handle feeling attacked and projects blame onto me, unknowingly.

We've had some tough years, of course, but our love is strong. So strong that after ten years of marriage we still haven't been able to separate. We are drawn to each other. Some days we work hard to be on the same page and to be understanding and patient. I know there are peaks and big valleys but I'm not giving up yet. Some days I wish I could be more accommodating and some days I wish he could just think like me and it would be so much easier. Every day I'm in a different place.

For our ten-year anniversary he surprised me with his own wedding ring. He had lost it and didn't wear one for years. It was very thoughtful when he showed me that he had gone out and bought one to show his dedication to our marriage during such tumultuous times. On the other hand, I was a little disappointed he didn't present me with anything. Not a card or a flower. He was so excited to show me what he had bought for himself. Although I was happy he was prioritizing our relationship, it felt funny for him to buy himself a gift and not me. I waited all day thinking he'd surprise me later in the day but that didn't happen. Looking back, I'm grateful that he wants to keep trying and that's all that matters. I'm looking forward to more positive days where we can be accepting of our differences.

* * *

River's comments:

SOMETIMES I THINK about how many of us have met our men on dating sites like Lauren and I did. I think about how, if I had selected the profile next to Gil's instead, my life would have been so different. But everything in life can be examined in that way when it comes down to it. What-ifs and shoulds and coulds are simple questions that bring unnecessary pain.

Lauren touched on something I really appreciate. In her first stages of dating, she saw the red flags straight away. "Something was off." "The communication didn't flow." "He acted childish." Etc. But the core values and what she wanted in a relationship were all there. Indeed, why break up with someone who is sometimes 'off' or childish or may have trouble communicating when the core beliefs and values are in place? The other stuff, and I hate to say that women generally look past those things, but we just might. In some cases, our eye is on the final goal of raising children or building a home together with someone. A man being awkward may not come off as a bad thing. Most of the time it may look endearing.

And it depends on the person. Gil showed confidence with his awkward side. Helped me to feel less intimidated. I know that I am still thrown by Gil's cuteness. His awkward, silly, and innocent nature at times. I want to sit him on my knee and read him a story because he is so cute. So yes, it is easy to overlook those things when we feel the major aspects we want in a relationship are there.

I am a foodie as well. Gil will eat most things but he doesn't like some of my favorite things. It is vital to find friends to share the things that your partner cannot share with you. And to know that it is totally okay to do so.

Lauren has learned to be more direct with her husband and that is key. We certainly need to be bilingual and learn their language, and to keep things simple for issues like showing up on time, getting tasks done, etc. I like to think of it like a recipe. When we need them to do something not in their realm, something for us directly, we have to be precise. We can't leave any detail out.

I remember in grade school when a teacher told us to find a partner. After we found our partner, she told us to choose which person will give the directions and which person will be directed. After we decided who would do what, she gave one person two pieces of bread, a cup of jelly, a cup of peanut butter and a plastic knife. The one giving directions was now to tell the person receiving directions how to make a PB and J sandwich. The person making the sandwich had to follow the directions precisely.

I remember my partner coming close to putting a piece of bread on his head because it was so hard to give directions precisely. I mean everyone knows how to make a PB and J right? So we have to think of specifics because when it comes to emotional decision making, our guys, for the most part, must have direct and precise instructions in order to understand. Not easy, because it comes so naturally to us.

I admire Lauren's courage and grit to keep going and move past betrayal and grief like she has. Often, we might look at the woman and wonder why she stays. How can she put up with it all? And I am here to say that I tremendously admire women who do work it out, as long as they stay true to themselves, and I see how Lauren has looked at what is real and what she can handle, and see love as truly conquering all. No matter the darkness, there is light and hope. She knows she needs to accept his differences. I too want Gil to think like me. I know that feeling all too well. Reality is key. Reality is freedom to *choose* to leave or stay. Reality is freedom from being the victim, and a chance at being the hero.

D. River Martin

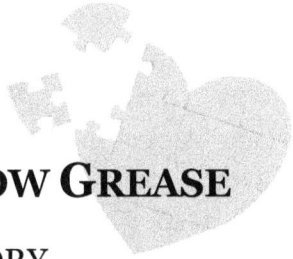

GRACE AND ELBOW GREASE

EVIE'S STORY

I AM EVIE. I'M IN MY TWENTIES and have been married to a man with high functioning autism for a year and a half. I'm part of a culture where women start dating for marriage at eighteen years old, but I wanted to end up with the right person, so I made sure to wait for marriage until I found someone who really clicked with me. I married my husband when I was twenty-two and he was twenty-six.

We dated long-distance and it was ten months from the time we met until the time we got married. I had dated some other guys before him, and a few of them had been on the autism spectrum. I had done my research on autism and I knew as soon as I started dating my husband what I was in for. At least, I thought I knew. My perception of people on the spectrum was very simple. I knew that some were very smart, they took words literally, had minimal social understanding, and altogether their brains operated differently than those who were not autistic.

My husband is very smart, funny, at the center of his group of friends, and extremely caring. I fell in

141

love with these qualities. I thought things like: "Oh, he has autism, but he's 'normal'. It just makes him extra smart." Or: "I don't understand why people make such a big deal over relationships with autistic partners, he's so wonderful and affectionate!"

It took a few months of marriage and living with him before I was able to fully grasp what life with an autistic spouse really was. It's days' worth of the silent treatment while he has (what we call) a meltdown. It's listening to the person I love rant for hours over something that most people would view as insignificant. It's living with someone with a very narrow-minded (in my husband's case, extremely pessimistic) view of the world and an almost complete inability to see outside of their perceptions. Occasionally it's crying myself to sleep at night because I feel like my partner can't understand me or what it takes to meet my needs.

Things that are routine for other couples, like kissing goodbye or saying goodnight, he deems 'unnecessary' and are therefore overlooked. Living with someone on the spectrum means giving over a part of yourself to accommodate their needs, and to work around their quirks.

Often, living with an autistic husband means dealing with their undiagnosed depression, anxiety, ADHD, and sensory issues. Sensory issues that make your spouse cringe when you try to touch them. A long list of sensory do's and don'ts begins to develop until your physical relationship feels so narrow that it stifles you. You can feel your world shrinking until all that's left is you, your husband, and all the quirky relationship problems that few people truly understand.

You crave validation that you are doing everything possible to keep your relationship alive and healthy, but you know that you will never get that from the one you love most, so you look outside the box. You find people in a similar situation and you begin to talk about what things are similar and what things are different.

I joined some Facebook support groups for partners of people on the spectrum and I learned that I have it pretty good compared to a lot of other relationships. My husband acknowledges that he is on the autism spectrum. We often joke that we speak English, but we are still speaking a foreign language to each other. Almost every conversation of substance takes five times longer than it should because of these brain barriers that we were born with. It takes so much patience on both ends to navigate this, and I know my husband struggles. But he continues to try because he wants our relationship to succeed.

I am lucky that my husband was diagnosed as a child because he acknowledges that his brain functions in a different way than mine. Because he was diagnosed early, being a high functioning autistic person just became a part of how he defines himself. His mother has always been extremely supportive of him and made sure to get him as much help as she could. I know he spent a lot of his childhood learning tools from his family, doctors, and teachers. He had to learn how to make eye contact in a conversation, studied facial expressions to try and understand what they meant, and learned how to socialize with others.

A lot of the social behavior that we take for granted, my husband spent years learning about. For example, someone with a neurotypical brain may see someone crying and automatically know that they are sad and might need some emotional support. For my husband, seeing someone crying is like putting together a puzzle. He processes it in steps.

1. I see someone crying.
2. Crying usually means that someone is sad.
3. Sad is an emotion that is not good.
4. I don't like that they are sad, what can I do?
5. Am I supposed to talk to them, hug them, bring them chocolate?

The thought process is extremely quick and it's ongoing for him. It is easy for him to get confused as well. For instance, if someone was crying out of happiness, he would have to recalibrate his step-by-step process and it will take him longer to understand what is happening and how he should react. He doesn't have many instincts about social behavior so everything he does is learned and calculated based on experience. He has a much easier time understanding his role in social situations when there is a 'rule' in place. For example, when you meet someone, you shake their hand. These unspoken rules need to be verbalized to him and then he can weave them into his social interactions.

My marriage may be difficult and fraught with weird problems, but at least my husband tries. My god, how he tries. He will put his last breath into trying to understand me. It is almost impossible for him to lie, so when he says he loves me and wants to continue working on our marriage, I really believe him. My husband is kind, honest, loyal, smart, and persistent. We may sometimes go days simmering in resentment and brewing over misunderstandings, but I know that my love will always return to me. He will try to work on himself, and he will thank me for my patience.

We will try to keep talking, we will try marriage counseling, and we will try all it takes to soldier on. Because no one else will ever try harder than my autistic husband.

~~~

Since writing about my experience over a year ago, a lot has changed in my relationship. My husband and I have gotten better at communicating, and are now able to understand each other a lot faster. It's been wonderful to improve our communication! We are a lot happier as a couple and recently welcomed our baby boy into the world. I feel very proud of myself and my husband for putting in the work to improve our relationship. I'm grateful to have him and his uniqueness in my life.

* * *

River's comments:

MY HEART MELTS reading Evie's words. When I heard from those who are young, and dating or married to men who were diagnosed at a young age, I felt a completely different take on things, which was very interesting and validated a lot of my hope for these couples. However, although her hubby was diagnosed at a young age and she knew going in—or at least felt that she knew—there were still struggles. And this makes sense because no matter what, as she put so perfectly, their brains work differently from each other's.

I take joy in reading about her love for him and how much he tries and truly does his best to understand their difficulties.

Wives/partners of autistic men who were not diagnosed young scramble to find answers, and wonder if they are crazy, and may be dealing with personality disorders along with the autism because of the damage caused to these men by being misunderstood. Maybe they were bullied for being different. Their family probably did not understand them and tried to make them be like everyone else. This can have long lasting effects on a person who is never diagnosed correctly, or at all.

A joke

Me: Alexa ... Blah blah blah

Alexa: I am having trouble understanding right now. Please try later.

Me: I'm so glad she is letting me know to please try

later.

I often wish Gil would let me know that I could try again later instead of blocking my requests altogether. It's a reflex for him due to his trouble dealing with any kind of change. We are working on that one. I only have to remind him and he tries.

2020

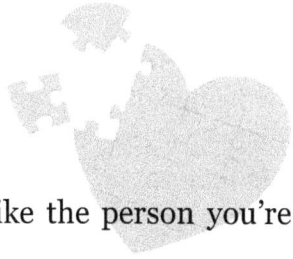

"You cannot be lonely if you like the person you're alone with."
(Wayne Dyer)

A FEW MONTHS AFTER LOCKDOWN, I had a fun Facetime call with a cousin of mine. She's in Peru and I'm in the States. We discussed the differences in both areas and what lockdown was like for us. When we got on the topic of life with our significant other and being cooped up in the house with them, she told me some of her experiences and asked me how it was for me with Gil. As soon as she asked, I could tell in her voice that she assumed it may have been rough. She is fully aware of his autism.

I said, "Oh gosh. It was a pleasant surprise. Believe it or not, I was the happiest I think I have ever been in my life during the initial three-month total lockdown in our state."

She was eager to find out more so I told her the whole story of what it was like.

When Gil and I heard the announcement on the television, we reacted as I am sure most would, with shock and many questions. "So, what's going to happen?" Even now, nine months later, we are still

149

asking "What's going to happen?"

Monday morning Gil set up shop to continue working from home. I, working with the school district at the time, saw no job in sight. As he set up his business room and I tried to figure out how to get unemployment, our worlds came together. Two worlds separate for so long finally came together. This put me in heaven! I couldn't express my joy to anyone because it's a pandemic. Not cool to be loving it right? People were dying. People lost their jobs. There was abuse in some homes, depression in others and here I was, blissfully happy. At first, I thought shock had set in deep. I had to be losing my mind to be so happy.

But I realized that I finally had Gil with me. He allowed me into his world because it was a time of inclusion. The only person he had to go to was me. And I could be wrong because he can't tell me why, but he's used to being 'on' during the day. I became like one of his employees and he had to wear that mask he tirelessly must wear in the outside world to keep his career.

I'll never forget my first grocery store run. I went by myself because he can't stand crowds. I waited in line and people everywhere were trying to get that last item on the shelf. I couldn't believe what was happening. The kind of thing you see on TV. I had my cloth gloves on, and no one was wearing masks. The first stages brought so much chaos and confusion.

After I got home, Gil helped me with the groceries, something he had never done before. As he put some things away for me, I sat on our living room chair and cried. He came over to me and I could feel that his presence was with me and that he could feel what I was feeling. He helped all that he could. With groceries all away, I tore off my clothes and took a shower. It was now popular to be germ phobic. I'd always naturally been that way anyway.

For two months Gil worked from home. I was in his schedule. 6 AM vegetable smoothie drink and breakfast. I made us homemade bread. 10 AM hot cup of tea, fifteen-minute break time. It was fun to have that break with him. I stayed on schedule with my writing. Those two months really got this book into motion! I felt supported by Gil. He saw that I stayed busy and didn't sit around all day eating bonbons. Lunch was fun to make for us. Dinner and bedtime felt relaxed and happy. We talked more. Gil was gentle when I told him I was afraid for my friend who thought she was sick with Covid. Luckily it was a false alarm. Gil shared with me what work was like. He made sure that when on a zoom call, I didn't walk by in my PJs. It was a very wonderful time.

The only things that Gil wasn't happy about were his slow internet and that he didn't want to shop alone. We did shop together. Otherwise, it would have been stressful. Everyone formed their strategies during lockdown. Got to keep sane. We had so much fun shopping together too. One time, we went in, we acted sneaky, Gil tugged at my pant belt and told me "Go! Go! Get the toilet paper!! I'll be right here. Hurry! Run!" I giggled all the way to the TP. There was enough by then, but he was so funny about it. I still laugh when I think about it.

We were very lucky that Gil was able to continue working. When the three months was up, he had an option to stay at home or go in. He chose to go in because of the slow internet. I didn't know how drastically things would go back to normal within a few days of him being back at work. The high of happiness was over. I had a kind of withdrawal. I remember I slept for almost two days. Depression set in, and I was even more lonely than before. But I kept writing and kept in touch with my online groups. I pulled through fine, but I miss that time so much.

Maybe when Gil retires, I can have him back again? But it won't be the same. I don't know what he will be like. What I do know is that the lockdown really opened my eyes. The ongoing invisible tension of being with him, and not being able to be in his world, is a constant strain. When I am in his world, I'm like a starved kitten left out in the cold and welcomed in for a dish full of warm milk.

Since I started writing this book, I created Zoom calls with women married to autistic men so that we can provide each other with much-needed support. It's a bit more personal than social media. We call them 'coffee chats' as they're very informal.

A few months after the lockdown, during one of my coffee chat calls, I asked the ladies how the lockdown was for them. The majority of ladies didn't tell me that it was horrible. Some had similar stories as mine; they felt so happy. I asked one of the ladies to share something difficult and she said she didn't want to jinx herself. Life was blissful! I asked her why so blissful. She said, "My hubby thinks the world's coming to an end, so he told me he was going to be nicer and he is being amazing."

Well dang it!! So, the only time women with these guys can be happy is if the world's coming to an end?

After receiving my second Covid vaccine, I experienced a significantly stronger reaction than with the first shot, as is expected. It was very difficult to sleep and my whole body ached. I felt an antsy kind of fatigue.

After a full day of sitting in a recliner, I felt the second night might be as difficult as the first. Gil was very gentle the first night, but it seemed he grew tired of my self-care. At one point he asked me if I had the flu, forgetting that it was the vaccine.

Gil had decided to take the next two days off from work, so he could stay up a bit later than he usually did. I felt it might be a good time to lie with him before bed and have him hold me. It would be the only time that I could have his arms around me during aches and pains with a small fever, since I wasn't contagious. I very much looked forward to lying next to him, but I kept my expectations to a minimum because I know he never wants to cuddle with me on a weekday.

On normal work nights, he reads before bed. I sometimes lie next to him while he reads in the dark with his Kindle and then, when he is ready for bed, he gets up and goes to the bathroom and I must skedaddle out of there by the time he comes back or I get the bright ceiling light turned on and he stands at the foot of the bed looking extremely frustrated that I am still there.

This time I lay there. I stayed. I thought, it's not a work night anyway, and I was feeling so very fatigued, like I could finally sleep. I didn't want to leave. It felt so heavenly lying there. His bed is fantastic, much better than mine. When he returned from the bathroom he turned on the bright light and stood there waiting.

I said, as I started to snicker because I knew what was happening, "You turned on the bright light to wake me up."

He grumpily said, "YES!"

I slowly got up as he stood there looking annoyed with me. I hugged him goodnight although I knew he was prickly because I didn't follow the schedule.

I felt a big smile grow on my face and I wanted to laugh. I thought, this is SO him right now. *This is how it is.* I don't think he heard me at all when I said I wanted to cuddle before bed. Yes, I will miss the one opportunity to feel comforted from feeling so physically crummy. Oh, how his bed felt good. Oh, how glorious it would have been to be held, lie next to him, and feel his body touching my achy, fatigued one.

He has spared no expense with his bed, mind you. The finest sheets and pillows to fight his insomnia. The cool breeze of his open window, as he makes it a perfect 68 degrees in his room before bed with our central fan.

I went right to bed, hoping to hold on to the heavily relaxed feeling I'd had. I lay down on my lonesome bed. My rough sheets and stuffy room with its closed window. I could have opened my windows but I'm afraid I might forget to close them and get his wrath if I don't. Due to those past experiences, I've lost the desire to open windows.

For a moment I wanted to go back to his room and force him to cuddle. My old way of doing things. But as I lay in bed, I thought of my book. I thought of how miraculous it truly is to understand him, finally. To keep from being triggered, like when I didn't know of his autism. If I didn't know, I would have begged him to lie with me. I would have felt hurt and angry and the overflowing feeling of despair would have kept me from getting the sleep I truly needed.

I slept a full nine hours. I awoke feeling good as new. When Gil woke up, I ran up to him and gave him a huge bear hug. He hugged back but I knew he was grumpy, and I didn't care. I am reminded once again of what a difference it makes to know that Gil is autistic and I am neurotypical, and we are both okay.

D. River Martin

WHEN WALLS COME CRASHING IN

I AM IN LOVE WITH A MAN WHO can't see me for who I really am. As I learn more and more about him, I get more and more hungry for answers because so often the literature leaves me with more questions.

"But what if he says or does this?" I ask. "What do I say to him and how do I care for a man that walks into fire and starts more fires?"

I feel so lost and dazed and sad at times. I feel he can't see me and how amazing I am. How much I love him. He often sees me as the enemy. He can't see it in my face when I'm sincere and fighting for us the way that I do.

I'm a complete fool in love, but it's lonely.

I want to run and go someplace but I can't because of the pandemic. But even if I had a place to go, I would come crawling back because so far, the good of being with him outweighs the bad.

Why do I fight so very much for him to maybe get a glimpse of me and who I am? If he had one moment to see me through non-autistic eyes, he would know how much I truly love him. I want his soul to see me. His spirit, that I love so deeply, to see me.

I'm a writer. I'm creative and love deeply. These are my strengths, and part of what caused me to fall in love with him. It's like heaven on earth when he puts me into his structured world of chaos and tenderness. The fight that he goes through every day, simply to make it through the day, I see whenever he comes near. I feel his struggle. He is aware of everything to a point that it all brings in too much noise. I feel he must drown it all out by focusing on a movie or his phone. The louder things are, the more the media drowns out all the small noises plaguing every moment of his life. He is sensitive to this world more than I will ever know. He is kind to all living creatures and he's like a beautiful child who holds that innocence so dear, when he wakes up in brief moments that are calm. Only to have the world squash it again.

I can't hide all the scars I have now. I can't allow life to slip by without fully enjoying his company and his worth in this world. I keep fighting for him and for our family even though I am an army of one. I simply want him to see me. See me for one moment, know that I am here for him and always will be. I'm deeply grateful that he is in my life. I will do whatever it takes to find more answers to my endless questions, and I will do all I can to keep us safe and happy. Even if I have not a fighting chance, I know that I've done the very best that I can possibly do.

ARTICLES AND RESOURCES

This isn't a scholarly book and I'm not trying to offer any kind of advice. However, it took me a long time to find websites with good information to help me understand my partner, so I'm sharing a few of them here. There are plenty more resources online but mostly, what partners of autistic people need is a good emotional support system, since our emotional needs can rarely be met by our partners.

https://kennethrobersonphd.com/adult-aspergers-and-the-cassandra-phenomena/

The Neurotypical Site
https://www.theneurotypical.com/effects-on-differing-nd-levels.html
This site shows a chart of the Effects of Differing Neuro/Developmental Levels on Neurotypical/ Autism Spectrum Adult Relationships

Good information on loneliness in a neuro-diverse relationship
https://www.goodtherapy.org/blog/how-to-deal-

with-loneliness-in-a-relationship-when-one-
partner-is-autistic-
1031194?fbclid=IwAR3UjEGLgnO_ZfNwSkkbrRyb
m_bhnbsn42kUZaUcp24OS2EIqsvK503U3g0

Good examples of the difference between a narcissist
and autism
http://www.drpsychmom.com/2015/08/28/asperge
rs-when-narcissism-just-doesnt-explain-your-
partners-inability-to-empathize

On theory of mind (mind blindness, or the inability to
put yourself in another person's shoes)
https://www.verywellmind.com/theory-of-mind-
4176826

Books:
Journal of Best Practices by David Finch

Videos:
Any of the Mark Hutten or Dr. Kathy Marshak videos
on YouTube

Good Video to explain high functioning autistic men
and why they can cover it up so well.
http://mixedneurological.com/?fbclid=IwAR3KhE1
_I_FGeEd2OizLQFXs_T8xYVE7Y6wTM4cSnaKhPj
aXhq-uuIuDjqY

www.aspergerpartner.com

ACKNOWLEDGEMENTS

I cannot find words to describe how much I appreciate my editor for helping me find the strength and courage to simply start this book. She encouraged me to write that first post in the Facebook group to find the contributors. Without her, there is no chance this book could have come together as beautifully as it has, despite the bumps and scrapes along the way. She not only encouraged me, she stuck by me during all the rough spots, often ironing them out with ease. I cannot ever thank her enough.

A very special thank you to all the contributors in this book. Without your vulnerability and willingness to completely open your hearts and your homes to us with your incredible stories, there wouldn't be a book. No glimpses into our often secret and misunderstood lives. I am deeply grateful for all of you. Your friendship, kindness, and trust mean the world to me. You are all simply incredible women!! Endless thanks to you all.

Thank you to an outstanding group of online supporters who listened to me when I had doubts and took time with me to help put together the finishing touches. I am forever grateful for your generous contribution.

Last but not least, my wonderful partner/forever fiancé, Gil. Without you, the notion of this book would not have existed. And, without you, I would not have had the time and energy to put this book into the world. Thank you, my darling.

www.ingramcontent.com/pod-product-compliance
Lightning Source LLC
Chambersburg PA
CBHW072010040426
42447CB00009B/1568